First World War
and Army of Occupation
War Diary
France, Belgium and Germany

37 DIVISION
Headquarters, Branches and Services
Royal Army Ordnance Corps
Deputy Assistant Director Ordnance Services
1 October 1915 - 30 April 1919

WO95/2520/1

The Naval & Military Press Ltd
www.nmarchive.com
Published in association with The National Archives

Published by

The Naval & Military Press Ltd

Unit 10 Ridgewood Industrial Park,

Uckfield, East Sussex,

TN22 5QE England

Tel: +44 (0) 1825 749494

www.naval-military-press.com

www.nmarchive.com

This diary has been reprinted in facsimile from the original. Any imperfections are inevitably reproduced and the quality may fall short of modern type and cartographic standards.

© **Crown Copyright**
Images reproduced by permission of The National Archives, London, England, 2015.

Contents

Document type	Place/Title	Date From	Date To
Heading	WO95/2520/1		
Heading	37th Division D.A.D.O.S. Sep 1915-Apr 1919		
Miscellaneous	37th Division H.Q. Less 37th Div. D.S.D.O.S. Vol I Sept 15 Apr 19		
Heading	War Diary Of Capt E.O. Cauison A.O.D. D.A.D.O.S. 37th Divn From 5.9.15 To 30.9.15		
War Diary	Pas	05/09/1918	30/09/1918
Heading	37th Division H.Q. 37th Div. D.A.D.O.S. Vol 2 Oct 15		
War Diary	Pas	01/10/1915	31/10/1915
Heading	H.Q. 37th Div. D.A.D.O.S. Vol 3 Nov 15		
War Diary	Pas	01/11/1915	30/11/1915
Heading	D.A.D.O.S. 37th Div. Vol 4		
War Diary	Pas	01/12/1915	31/12/1915
Heading	D.A.D.O.S. 37th Division War Diary For Month Of January 1916		
War Diary	Pas	01/01/1916	31/01/1916
Heading	D.A.D.O.S. 37th Div. Vol 5		
Heading	War Diary For February 1916 37th Div 29.2.16		
War Diary	Pas	01/02/1916	20/02/1916
War Diary	Bavincourt	21/02/1916	29/02/1916
Heading	C.2118 D.A.D.O.S. 37th Division (Capt. W.D. Harbinson) War Diary For March 1916		
War Diary	Bavincourt	01/03/1916	19/03/1916
War Diary	Ficheux	20/03/1916	26/03/1916
War Diary	Lucheux	27/03/1916	31/03/1916
Heading	War Diary For April 1916 37th Div. 2.5.16 D.A.D.O.S. 37 Vol 8		
War Diary	Lucheux	01/04/1916	30/04/1916
Heading	War Diary For May 1916 37th Div. D.O.D.O.S. 37 Div. Vol 9		
War Diary	Lucheux	01/05/1916	03/05/1916
War Diary	Bavincourt	04/05/1916	31/05/1916
Heading	D.A.D.O.S. 37th Division War Diary For June 1916 D A D O S 37 Div Vol		
War Diary	Bavincourt	01/06/1916	09/06/1916
War Diary	Abincourt	10/06/1916	18/06/1916
War Diary	Bavincourt	19/06/1916	01/07/1916
Heading	War Diary Of D.A.D.O.S. 37th Div. For July 1916		
War Diary	Bavincourt	01/07/1916	03/07/1916
War Diary	Pas	04/07/1916	18/07/1916
War Diary	Bruay	19/07/1916	31/07/1916
Heading	C. 2118 War Diary For August 1916 D.A.D.O.S. Vol 12	31/08/1916	31/08/1916
War Diary	Bruay	01/08/1916	31/08/1916
Heading	D.A.D.O.S. 37th Div. War Diary For September 1916 Vol 13		
War Diary	Bruay	01/09/1916	06/09/1916
War Diary	In The Field	06/09/1916	10/09/1916
War Diary	Bruay	11/09/1916	18/09/1916
War Diary	Barlin	19/09/1916	30/09/1916

Type	Location	Start	End
Heading	D.A.D.O.S. 37th Division War Diary For October 1916 Vol 14		
Heading	October 1916		
War Diary	Barlin	01/10/1916	18/10/1916
War Diary	Rollecourt	18/10/1916	19/10/1916
War Diary	Lecauroy	20/10/1916	20/10/1916
War Diary	Marieux	21/10/1916	31/10/1916
Heading	War Diary For November 1916 37th Division 24.12.16 Vol 15	24/12/1916	24/12/1916
War Diary	Marieux	01/11/1916	15/11/1916
War Diary	Hedauville	16/11/1916	16/11/1916
War Diary	Forceville	17/11/1916	25/11/1916
War Diary	Forceville Marieux	26/11/1916	26/11/1916
War Diary	Marieux	27/11/1916	30/11/1916
Heading	War Diary For D.A.D.O.S. 37 Division For December 1916 Vol 16		
War Diary	Marieux	01/12/1916	13/12/1916
War Diary	Frohen-Le-Grand	14/12/1916	14/12/1916
War Diary	Bethune	15/12/1916	21/12/1916
War Diary	Lestrem	22/12/1916	24/12/1916
War Diary	In The Field	25/12/1916	31/12/1916
Heading	War Diary 37th Division Period Month Ending 31st January 1917 Vol 17 3rd February 1917 D.A.D.O.S. 37th Division		
War Diary	In The Field	01/01/1917	05/01/1917
War Diary	Letrem	05/01/1917	31/01/1917
Heading	37th Division War Diary For Month Ending 28th February 1917 Vol 18 2nd March 1917 D.A.D.O.S. 37th Division	02/03/1917	02/03/1917
War Diary	Lestrem	01/02/1917	12/02/1917
War Diary	Braquemont	13/02/1917	28/02/1917
Heading	37th Division War Diary For Month Ending 31st March 1917 Vol 19		
War Diary	Braquemont	01/03/1917	04/03/1917
War Diary	Braquemont Norrent Fontes	04/03/1917	04/03/1917
War Diary	Roellecourt	05/03/1917	31/03/1917
Heading	37th Division War Diary For Month Ending 30th April 1917 Vol 20		
War Diary	Rollecourt	01/04/1917	04/04/1917
War Diary	Agnes Les Duisans	05/04/1917	13/04/1917
War Diary	Lignereuil	14/04/1917	20/04/1917
War Diary	Etrun	21/04/1917	25/04/1917
War Diary	Arras	26/04/1917	29/04/1917
War Diary	Lignereuil	30/04/1917	30/04/1917
Heading	37th Division War Diary For Month Ending 31st May 1917 Vol 21 37th Division		
War Diary	Lignereuil	01/05/1917	18/05/1917
War Diary	Warlus	19/05/1917	20/05/1917
War Diary	Arras	21/05/1917	31/05/1917
Heading	37th Division War Diary For Month Ending 30th June 1917 Vol 22 D.A.D.O.S. 37		
War Diary	Arras	01/06/1917	01/06/1917
War Diary	Lignereuil	02/06/1917	07/06/1917
War Diary	Bomy	08/06/1917	22/06/1917
War Diary	Steenbecque	23/06/1917	23/06/1917
War Diary	Dranoutre	24/06/1917	30/06/1917

Heading	37th Division War Diary From Month Ending 31st July 1917 Vol 23		
War Diary	Dranoutre	01/07/1917	31/07/1917
Heading	37th Division War Diary For Month Ending 31st August 1917 37th Division Vol 24		
War Diary	Dranoutre	01/08/1917	07/08/1917
War Diary	Locre	08/08/1917	31/08/1917
Heading	37th Division War Diary For Month Ending 30th September 1917 37th Division Vol 25		
War Diary	Locre	01/09/1917	11/09/1917
War Diary	St. Vans Cappel	12/09/1917	27/09/1917
War Diary	Dezon Camp	28/09/1917	30/09/1917
Heading	37th Division War Diary For Month Ending 31st October 1917 Vol 26 37th Division		
War Diary	Dezon Camp	01/10/1917	14/10/1917
War Diary	St. Jans Cappel	15/10/1917	31/10/1917
Heading	War Diary For November 1917 Vol 27		
War Diary	St. Jans Cappel	01/11/1917	09/11/1917
War Diary	Locre	10/11/1917	11/11/1917
War Diary	Sherpenberg	12/11/1917	22/12/1917
War Diary	Scherpenberg	23/11/1917	30/11/1917
Heading	D.A.G. 3rd Echelon		
War Diary	Sherpenberg	01/12/1917	10/01/1918
War Diary	Blaringhem	11/01/1918	31/01/1918
Heading	War Diary For February 1918 From. D.A.D.O.S. 37th Division		
War Diary	Blaringhem	01/02/1918	16/02/1918
War Diary	Westoutre	17/02/1918	26/02/1918
War Diary	Dickebush	27/02/1918	28/02/1918
Heading	War Diary For March 1918 From D.A.D.O.S. 37th Division		
War Diary	Dickebusch	01/03/1918	20/03/1918
War Diary	Westoutre	21/03/1918	28/03/1918
War Diary	Westoutre-Flesselles	29/03/1918	29/03/1918
War Diary	Flesselles-Pas	30/03/1918	30/03/1918
War Diary	Pas	31/03/1918	01/04/1918
Heading	War-Diary For April 1918 Vol 32 From D.A.D.O.S. 37th Division.		
War Diary	Pas	01/04/1918	01/04/1918
War Diary	Pas Couin	02/04/1918	02/04/1918
War Diary	Couin	03/04/1918	15/04/1918
War Diary	Authie	16/04/1918	23/04/1918
War Diary	Pas	24/04/1918	30/04/1918
Heading	D.A.G. 3rd Echelon War Diary Of D.A.D.O.S. 37th Div For Month Of May & June 1918		
Miscellaneous	Indent for Ordn?		
War Diary	Pas	01/05/1918	05/06/1918
War Diary	Cavillon	06/06/1918	10/06/1918
War Diary	Nailly	11/06/1918	21/06/1918
War Diary	Pas	22/06/1918	30/06/1918
Heading	War Diary Of DADOS 37th Div. For Month Of July 1918		
Miscellaneous			
War Diary	Pas	01/07/1918	31/07/1918
Miscellaneous	Diary Of DADOS 37th Division For Month Of August 1918		

War Diary	Pas	01/08/1918	16/08/1918
War Diary	Henu	17/08/1918	24/08/1918
War Diary	Fonquevillers	25/08/1918	29/08/1918
War Diary	Achiet-Le-Grand	30/08/1918	31/08/1918
Heading	D.A.D.O.S. 37th Div. Vol 6		
Heading	D.A.G. 3rd Ech		
War Diary	Achiet-Le-Grand	01/09/1918	07/09/1918
War Diary	Favreuil	08/09/1918	11/09/1918
War Diary	Velu	12/09/1918	13/09/1918
War Diary	Velu	14/09/1918	14/09/1918
War Diary	Labucquiere	15/09/1918	19/09/1918
War Diary	Vermelles	10/10/1918	10/10/1918
War Diary	Hancourt	11/10/1918	22/10/1918
War Diary	Caudry	23/10/1918	29/10/1918
War Diary	Briastre	30/10/1918	31/10/1918
Heading	War Diary November 1918 D.A.D.O.S. 37th Division	30/11/1918	30/11/1918
War Diary	Briastre	01/11/1918	05/11/1918
War Diary	Neuville	06/11/1918	10/11/1918
War Diary	Caudry	11/11/1918	30/11/1918
Heading	War Diary For December 1918 Vol 40 From D.A.D.O.S. 37th Division.	02/01/1919	02/01/1919
War Diary	Caudry	01/12/1918	01/12/1918
War Diary	Gommegnies	02/12/1918	15/12/1918
War Diary	Gosselies	16/12/1918	31/12/1918
Heading	War Diary For January 1919 D.A.D.O.S. 37th Division	01/02/1919	01/02/1919
War Diary	Gosselies	01/01/1919	30/01/1919
Heading	War Diary For February 1919 Deputy Assistant Director Of Ordnance Service 37th Division		
War Diary	Gosselies	20/02/1919	28/02/1919
Heading	War Diary For February 1919 Deputy Assistant Director Of Ordnance Service 37th Division		
Heading	War Diary For March 1919 From D.A.D. Ordnance 37 Division		
War Diary	Gosselies	01/03/1919	31/03/1919
Heading	War Diary For April 1919 From D.A.D.O.S. 37th Division		
War Diary	Gosselies	01/04/1919	21/04/1919
Heading	War Diary For April 1919 From. D.A.D.O.S. Brabant Sub-Area (No. 4 Area)		
War Diary	Gosselies	22/04/1919	30/04/1919
Heading	War Diary For April 1919 From D.A.D.O.S. Brabant Sub-Area (no. 4 Area)		
Heading	War Diary For April 1919 From D.A.D.O.S. 37th Division		

37TH DIVISION

D. A. D. O. S.
SEP 1915-APR 1919

13/
6920.

37th Division

Ad: Gen: 37th Div:
Basel.

vol I
Sep. 15
ap 19

Confidential

War Diary
of
Capt. E. O. Hollison, A.O.D.
D.A.D.O.S. 37th Divn.

From 5.9.15. to 30.9.15.

Army Form C. 2118.

WAR DIARY
or
INTELLIGENCE SUMMARY.
(Erase heading not required.)

Instructions regarding War Diaries and Intelligence Summaries are contained in F.S. Regs., Part II. and the Staff Manual respectively. Title pages will be prepared in manuscript.

Place	Date	Hour	Summary of Events and Information	Remarks and references to Appendices
Div	5/9		Arrived from Scotland with Advance Party of Divnl and shipped my Office in the Hotel de Ville. Reported arrival to D.D.O.S. 3rd Army.	See
	6/9		Obtained sanction for Divisional Forge. On location of Div Engs. they showed sands suitable for Divisional Forge. Sent to G.H.Q. for Div Service Chaplains.	See
	7/9		Attached to 2nd R.E. for employ. Enlisted men for Divisional Workshops from Div Engr Shops formed a ground floor of Hotel de Ville. These men were obtained from the Infantry Battalions of the Division. The set of tools and also supplies of each Battalion Workshop supplied an amount from the Base.	See
	8/9		Visit of Maj. of M.T. Infantry Brigade. Since arrival at the Head of D.D.O.S 3rd Army — Inspection of Workshops Staff at Head Qrs. I have consulted the whole of my Brigade M.O. Continue to effort to clean their own to Stock — with out the above to refitting boots.	See

T2134. Wt. W708—776. 500000. 4/15. Sir J. C. & S.

WAR DIARY or INTELLIGENCE SUMMARY

Army Form C. 2118.

(Erase heading not required.)

Instructions regarding War Diaries and Intelligence Summaries are contained in F. S. Regs., Part II. and the Staff Manual respectively. Title pages will be prepared in manuscript.

Place	Date	Hour	Summary of Events and Information	Remarks and references to Appendices
Pad	8/9		Stores arrive at Railhead usually four daily - this is not sufficient as frequently the lorries are employed at Spitzkop bridge - when they are also required at the Railhead	See Enc /
	9/9		No remarks	
			Arrival of Rhod Regmt to replace a similar number withdrawn Imp Inf Bn R.B. 1643. Horses to C.I.B. 3rd Army Bde	See /
			Visited units of 12th Brigade.	
			Part of R.E. of 37th Drivers the isolated workshops 2072 proceed to Omburn to purchase camps with colored guided for directing cooking fires at night - 12 regards by each Infantry Brigade - also purchased material for mixing bread & employing Natl Carpenters for this - both provided by unit.	
			Bill Consignment of blankets received & distributed - weather See Enc	
	10/9		Further Consignment of blankets received & issued. Purchased the number of horses (60 Farm) for storing drinking water in the trenches - See 13 Frome and	See /

WAR DIARY
or
INTELLIGENCE SUMMARY.

Army Form C. 2118.

Place	Date	Hour	Summary of Events and Information	Remarks and references to Appendices
Poo	13/9		Has been asked to provide suitable portable wooden bozes for keeping infant rations hot in the trenches. Have sampled one borrowed from supply. Liked idea, the depth of which is needed to admit of a large brick, but of a handier kind. Have placed order — sent South Command made stopped with half, the whole supposed to front line carriers. Asked GOC were material available. Begins task. Chaplains with Quartermasters + Brig. Majors of mils: arranged a reserve with instructions issued by Lt-Col. J.P.S., 3rd Army. Representatives from all mils. attended. Students were reviewed with a view to-concealing any outstanding items as longer required. Purchased cabs. Qanveh of command regimen of RTO Batteries for issue to Qm employments. Fine, 1 borne to End. for mats. Record around 2,710 inter ballon sortie helmet from G.R.P.B. 3rd Army	AC DA
	15/9			AC DA

Army Form C. 2118.

WAR DIARY
or
INTELLIGENCE SUMMARY.
(Erase heading not required.)

Instructions regarding War Diaries and Intelligence Summaries are contained in F.S. Regs., Part II. and the Staff Manual respectively. Title pages will be prepared in manuscript.

Place	Date	Hour	Summary of Events and Information	Remarks and references to Appendices
Q10	16/9		Eight West Kent now arrived 6. Brigade in the trenches	302
	17/9		Visited Bge Hd. Qrs – Field Coys R.E. 6th are a few Sergeants. Stated that entrenchment Coke is not taken by units 6 present relief – In advance have their own engineers returned when only part covers – Demanded ten men per Coy to work to barrel of saddle pair and to repair tools – Spoke to Bg Steven Hennessy to also explain to Offrs idea of Equipment. Have had a circular letter to this effect published.	200 / 250
	18/9 19/9		No Events. Visited Brigade Hd Qd 110th, 111th, 1712 Infantry Brigades. An emis– outting supply of Spare parts for Lewis Machine Guns & full Armament of Machine (64) per Sam – have taken all necessary action to obtain	300
	20/9		Authorised by G.O.C. to congrat. H.P. & ??? Copes (Comm: 9 Corps) for storming of Wali: on he finished. This 9th Sch Inf:	300 / 302

T2124. Wt. W703—776. 500000. 4/15. Sir J. C. & S.

WAR DIARY
or
INTELLIGENCE SUMMARY.

Army Form C. 2118.

Place	Date	Hour	Summary of Events and Information	Remarks and references to Appendices
Pos.	22/9		Instructed by G.O.C. to ascertain during quantity of 15mm Ordnance shells to be issued to us to get larger allotment to trenches for the purpose of illumin: [illegible] from held. One of Orders 1½ mile = 3 Star to mile. Considered fire of musketry (3.50 Secs) must be sufficient - was suitable until Ados Car to improvised from first trials.	See
	22/9		Purchased yellow material under instructions of O.C. for issue to Infantry Battalions - about 6 Square yd per Battalion for developing artillery fire.	See
	23/9		Received further consignment of Ivance Sprayers. The total now received is 50. Also received some copies of G.O.C. instructions for Battalion to be Kept in company water to 194th Brigade.	See
	24/9		Visited 110th Infantry Brigade also 19th Brigade Rifles & 9th North Stafford Regt.	See

WAR DIARY
or
INTELLIGENCE SUMMARY

Army Form C. 2118.

Place	Date	Hour	Summary of Events and Information	Remarks and references to Appendices
Sho	23/9		Inspected men of Bronor. All work are now complete with exception of Tube Station Which gave Ordinary Work for Officers men and Ten Ordinary Work for Other Men & Divisional Res.	30/c 20/c
	26/9		Visited Work on Site. No work.	
	27/9		No Work.	
	28/9		Visited 110th Infantry Brigade H.Q. Layer W. Work left no work for clothing.	
			Observed Unused for Clothing.	30/c
			Representatives from each attended fortnightly Conference.	
	29/9		Visit of D.A. & D. 3rd Army, who inspected workshops & Camps.	
	30/9		Observed all Reported to have all work having been completed with Two Ordinary Extra Snipers Little.	30/c

30/9.

E. Milliken Capt
D.A. D.A.Q 37 Div.

37th Division

H.Q. 37th Div: A.A.S.O.L.
vol: 2
Oct 15

Army Form C. 2118.

WAR DIARY
or
INTELLIGENCE SUMMARY.

(Erase heading not required.)

D.H.Q. Nov 37 5151

Instructions regarding War Diaries and Intelligence Summaries are contained in F. S. Regs., Part II. and the Staff Manual respectively. Title pages will be prepared in manuscript.

Place	Date	Hour	Summary of Events and Information	Remarks and references to Appendices
PHS	1/10		Worked locally under—	See
	2/10		Visited 13th Brigade R.F.A. & 78th Bde R.F.A. also 110th & 112th Sig. Sec. Shortage of Bugle Note reported by 3" Battery not Bdr Alexander R.F.A. an intelligent man has been met to deal—	See
	3/10		No movement.	
	4/10		R.O.C. authorised the purchase of 20 most Carts for holding mules in the Hospital. Also 16 additional clamps to be made by Infantry. The Divisional Artillery etc. The Clamps are placed under instruction of lighting made from local timber having three Coloured Shades. The Gutter were made in Divisional Armourers Shop	See
	5/10		Purchased a further Quantity of material for making boots, dage ease. Engined & boots returned by units for repair. I am forced it necessary to transfer 150 pairs of boots to the bode for repair being unable to cope with the amount of work to be done.	See

Army Form C. 2118.

WAR DIARY
or
INTELLIGENCE SUMMARY.
(Erase heading not required.)

Place	Date	Hour	Summary of Events and Information	Remarks and references to Appendices
P.H.S.	6/10		No Entry.	
	7/10		Visited 110th, 111th & 112th Infantry Brigades also 7th Br. Lincolns Regt. Approved of the erection of a Camp to be used as a bath for 1st Bn. Footlers, 1/6th Bn. N. Staff Regt., 50,000.	See
	8/10		Visited 8th Bn. East Lancs Regt. Inspected trenches from Experiment with a view to ascertaining requirements of Expert party. 8th Bn. 10th Br. L.N. Lancs Regt. established a school for 500 Coys each to replace those tasked inadequate, those to experience of Company Reported to a letter to R.A.S.M.O. who was asked for report re situation. This unit had been previously reported for insufficient clothing all a failure of suitable requirements. No remedies under consideration made by the D.D.M.S. - Obtained about a loss of winter comfortable for men in trenches. Ex supply necessary of Canvas Covers for rifles as now being made up by the 2nd Battalion in reserve to Infantry Battalion for protection of	See DDC

WAR DIARY
or
INTELLIGENCE SUMMARY.
(Erase heading not required.)

Army Form C. 2118.

Place	Date	Hour	Summary of Events and Information	Remarks and references to Appendices
Pys	10/10		rifles in the trenches. We even hear shell of ourselves cracking overhead. Germans snipers & situp lovely over about 800 yards.	DOC
	11/10		Fouled mid- by H.Q. My Bde in the trenches. This and all the usual intricating. French soldiers appeared to be panic - about 30 of our Battalion have been somewhat with them. Very possible. French rifle shells are also newer. Guns stored about 1/2 - practically were used on our front. In the trenches.	DOC
	12/10		Fortnightly Conference of Bn. Comdrs & Adjuts. Representatives from all units attached to "Bde" were also present. Certain alters expressly required the were orderly to the hospital.	DOC
	13/10		Posted III to Infantry Brigade. A Lieut in place from a Bay Shout Range Finder (Goerz) in charge of St Luidan Regt. destroyed by shell fire - tried to have mounted antly of same to replace - no answer yet	DOC / DOC
	14/10			

WAR DIARY
or
INTELLIGENCE SUMMARY.
(Erase heading not required.)

Army Form C. 2118.

Place	Date	Hour	Summary of Events and Information	Remarks and references to Appendices
PAB	15/10		Visited 184th Brigade 27th obs. 110th & 110th Infantry Brigades. Received news machine guns & 1562 p.m. were handed over to 8th Russian Regt	
	16/10		Received word from Attitude to Montdiament. Working a plan for saddlers sewing machine since too few — this will help considerably as hand machine have to be slower. Received 176 French stretchers	Soc Soc
	17/10		Report of ambulance of enquiry proposing 29 Visited 11th Infantry Bde of French Regt. Two additional Shaving penaths Letts formed for duty with Divisional troops. The establishment is now 8. Visited units of 111 Infantry Brigade.	Soc Soc Soc
	18/10			
	19/10		No remarks	
	20/10		Bosl. Beddard received for 296 Inf-CHR. Distribution will be made to units to Armour of Corps.	Soc

WAR DIARY or INTELLIGENCE SUMMARY

Army Form C. 2118.

(Erase heading not required.)

Place	Date	Hour	Summary of Events and Information	Remarks and references to Appendices
P.a.S.	2/10		No move. Rd	JoC
	3/10		Visit 103rd Bde H.Q. who O/take Bde 110th Inf Bde 9711 Inf Bde. Position of two Bns reported. Served with Curry in rear Only 200 supplies from Base east of a thousand for 1500	JoC
	3/10		Purchased 16 Lungs required by Sepoys Reinforces for those who received two new Kulmi peshks + two morning shirts	JoC
	4/10		Observed movements of Hindu clothing	JoC
			Visit Head Quarters M.O. Received Inst Bde Drivers Inst patterns blankets. These have been distributed to Indian Infantry of the Division	JoC
	7/10		No remarks	JoC
	26/10		Reproachable firms all into attached fortnightly conference Indents were received quota made of Items which are reported for issued the cancellation of outstanding indents.	JoC
			Upon being asked to make about 1000 Bombs carried	
	27/10		of B Head Pullipar 2500 yds of Cannel Leaser Known chaps	

Place	Date	Hour	Summary of Events and Information	Remarks and references to Appendices
FHQ	28/10		From Ostrowo Hars. The 107TR will be billeted by Sight. Victory to be supplied by Battalion.	See Sec
	29/10		Vooli 194². Bde R/Qrs abs. 110².Inf. Bde S. 111 Inf. Bde. Purchased 46 horse Nato (66 Pmts) for charge of Bombers in 5/th finished under Liute of R.A.O. Staboffz Lobracki and Skopacz must be ready to be trained to Brigade of 11.08	See
	30/10		Har. Gren Ate to the notice of the A.A.Drs that Civilian inhabitants are still returning here shots which are far from being warmed out. A special Order on the subject has been published to be strictly obeyed.	See See
	31/10		No remark.	

Johnson Cope
DHP 21 37 in

31/10

12/751

No. 37 L Bii:
Castings
Vol 3
Nov. 15

WAR DIARY or INTELLIGENCE SUMMARY

Army Form C. 2118

Place	Date	Hour	Summary of Events and Information	Remarks and references to Appendices
P.H.Q.	1/11		Various units of 110th Infy Bde.	
	2/11		Staff Capt. Fishman transferred to 51st Div. for mobilization into D.A.D.O. for appointment to Brigade H.Q. Reserve Ammunition Co. responsible for boots + clothing. Indents put forward by Brigade — 9950 instead of arrange at Amiens for 120 Prenels for ex 119 Inf. Bde. Brigade Laundry. Brig. to arrange for washing have decided to make up as many as possible a laundry shop. Canvas wrapping from clothing is suitable for washing. Can turn out about 550 pr. per wk.	90
	3/11		Major Serg. B. Skyber temporarily attached for duty, left for Rouen in return to Ordnance Coy. Lieut Somset. Army D.A.D.O. 3rd Army. Millinery Conference held in Officers D.A.D.Os Army. Arrangements were made for the distribution of certain stores left by the Divisions. Am instructed to make up disturbance for the command of 9 crosses for all units. 1557th additional men will be employed in disinfect shop.	90
	4/11			90

WAR DIARY
or
INTELLIGENCE SUMMARY.
(Erase heading not required.)

Army Form C. 2118

Instructions regarding War Diaries and Intelligence Summaries are contained in F.S. Regs., Part II. and the Staff Manual respectively. Title pages will be prepared in manuscript.

Place	Date	Hour	Summary of Events and Information	Remarks and references to Appendices
Pul.	5/11		Visited 110th, 111th, 112th, by Bn. 113 bat. Bde. Try large numbers of huts required to replace motorcycle cars & to shelter & continue wet weather — all animals have been out. This winter has been miserable continue. The Divisional Photographic Shop — about 60 pcs of huts have been required daily during the past three weeks.	See Top.
	6/11		No remarks	
	7/11		Received 1500 pond from bags thigh: five years have been issued to 1st Sargh. 110 & 112; 2nd Bde Brigade 100 pairs to — Rifle Bn this; not 150 pairs will for the present Kept in Store for 153 & 154 — field boots — R.E. and Entries sent to the Z.O.O. who	See
	8/11		On inspection of Equipment affected or charge to 112 -- appeared satisfactory --	&c
	9/11		Fortnightly conference of Quarter Masters Q.M. for Supply — held to-day. I think Forward Works looked whilst were urgently required —	OoQ

T2134. Wt. W708—776. 500000. 4/15. Sir J. C. & S.

WAR DIARY
or
INTELLIGENCE SUMMARY.
(Erase heading not required.)

Place	Date	Hour	Summary of Events and Information	Remarks and references to Appendices
	10/11		Visited 110th, 111th & 112th Infantry Brigades -	See
	11/11		No march.	
	12/11		Visited R.H.A. unit. Several batteries complain of unsuitable clothing transport from Batterie. Gifts by Division.	See
			Also some difficulty expected.	
	13/11		C.R.A. of 4th Division with reference to Z above. Informed G.O.C. Brigade orders for all items of Equipment which has issued, and to Arrangements for issue & preparing charges when will be made to Cost/Losses.	See
	14/11		Visited 16th Heavy Brigade R.G.A. – Issued 440 pairs Shirtpants & R.D. mix.	See
	15/11		No marches.	
	16/11		Visited 110th, 111th & 112th Infantry Brigades. Issued a further 600 pairs of fur bags to Infantry units.	See
	17/11		Visited 4th Divisional Ammunition.	See

WAR DIARY
or
INTELLIGENCE SUMMARY

Army Form C. 21

Place	Date	Hour	Summary of Events and Information	Remarks and references to Appendices
Pas	18/11		Visit of B.G.G.S. 3rd Army – Received further consignment of Sniper Stores 9/8 August	SoS
	19/11		Demanded 2nd Blankets for all units of the Division – Received further consignment (210) of knee boots thigh	GoC
	20/11		No remarks	
	21/11		Received & distributed a further consignment of 2100 pairs of knee boots thigh. It was thought to relieve G.O.C. artillery that a number of serviceable articles of clothing have been returned as irreparable. Units Comr. have had some reminders sent.	SoS G/a GoC SoS
	22/11		No remarks	
	23/11		Visited Brigade Hd. Qrs. 110, 111, 7/12 Infantry Brigades. No remarks.	
	24/11		Lieut. C.F.J. Ratcliffe joined for duty.	
	25/11		Inspected Umbs. of 110 Infantry Brigade – Received a further consignment of Anti-Gas Boggles – Was to – date ...?	GoC

Army Form C. 2118.

WAR DIARY
or
INTELLIGENCE SUMMARY.
(Erase heading not required.)

Instructions regarding War Diaries and Intelligence Summaries are contained in F. S. Regs., Part II. and the Staff Manual respectively. Title pages will be prepared in manuscript.

Place	Date	Hour	Summary of Events and Information	Remarks and references to Appendices
Pas.	26/11		Visited 110th, 111th, 112th Brigades after inspecting the new Wilting Depot at St. Amand, established for the purpose of preventing congestion of traffic. Also visited the trenches occupied by 13th K.R.R's but in the small area of its front going line to which I went I noted an entire absence of gum boots, although the issue of them had been made to cover all needs. On the other hand I have no reason to doubt that men were properly equipped elsewhere.	G.O.C. S.O.
"	27/11		No remarks.	
"	28/11		Visited O.O. Railhead in connection with the recent order concerning his signature to Way Bills. Subsequently endeavoured to obtain shoe makers for repairs in Divisional Boot Shop and with this had in view paid visits to 50th & 58th Field Ambulance, 123rd Bde. R.F.A., and Hd. Qrs. 110. Infy. Bde. A further consignment of 2300 Blankets came to hand in part completion of issue of second blanket to troops.	S.O. S.O.C.
"	29/11		No remarks	
"	30/11		Visited D.D.O.S. III Army with reference to Departmental duties.	

Ö.A.D.D. 37½ sti:
bet: 4

12/7936

Bros

Army Form C. 2118.

WAR DIARY
or
INTELLIGENCE SUMMARY.
(Erase heading not required.)

Instructions regarding War Diaries and Intelligence Summaries are contained in F. S. Regs., Part II. and the Staff Manual respectively. Title pages will be prepared in manuscript.

Place	Date	Hour	Summary of Events and Information	Remarks and references to Appendices
Pas.	1/12		Visited Amiens for the purpose of making local purchases authorized by G.O.C. 37th Divn. Also submitted records of such issues for the month of November to D.D.O.S. IIIrd Army, and indent for Cable & Telephones to D.C. Signal Co.	See App [?]
	2/12		See transports. See Lord Wallace's inspector Army in reply of Lieut. Robertson.	See App [?]
	3/12		Visited 111th Infy Bde also 111 & 112th Brigades. Received for the Consignment of Blankets (2nd issue) also sub-western & Capse distributed.	See App [?]
			Demand for clothing troops during the past month have been very heavy. This is partly due to the fact that a good deal of clothing in the Division had become irreplaceable at the time. Officers Commanding units have been asked to exert a strict watchfulness to keep it in careful order on mend – For in consequence of an increased effort in the Divisional forge than requires the use of another forge. The number of men now employed in making horse shoes is 10.	See App [?]
	4/12		Visited 139th & 1st D.H.F. Brigade R.F.A. also some workshops.	See App [?]

Army Form C. 2118.

WAR DIARY
or
INTELLIGENCE SUMMARY.
(Erase heading not required.)

Instructions regarding War Diaries and Intelligence Summaries are contained in F. S. Regs., Part II. and the Staff Manual respectively. Title pages will be prepared in manuscript.

Place	Date	Hour	Summary of Events and Information	Remarks and references to Appendices
	7/12		Fortnightly conference of Quartermasters. Shortage of tools, reviewed. Shortage of tools, pantaloons & caps reported by all units. Neatest supply from Ords.	SOC
	8/12		Received & issued a further consignment of 5mm boots high 15- 110/- & 711 Infantry Brigade. 500 pairs issued to the former & 160 to the latter.	SOC / SOC
	9/12		No remarks	
	10/12		Part of 9th & 31st Army Inspected Workshops. Visited 111 & 719 & Infantry Brigade. Large number of small repairs required to boots in the trenches. Redemption Coy. made up & ready, supply out.	SOC / SOC
	11/12		Frames was hopped for the men.	
	12/12		No remarks.	
	13/12		Received stores tongh Preston 200 - Issued 15 three Infantry Brigade on trial. Also received and issued a further consignment of sheepskin 348-	SOC / SOC
	14/12		No remarks	

Army Form C. 2118.

WAR DIARY
or
INTELLIGENCE SUMMARY.
(Erase heading not required.)

Instructions regarding War Diaries and Intelligence Summaries are contained in F. S. Regs., Part II. and the Staff Manual respectively. Title pages will be prepared in manuscript.

Place	Date	Hour	Summary of Events and Information	Remarks and references to Appendices
Pd	15/11		No remarks.	
	16/12		Visited Central mob. Board. had a number of vehicles previously. Lt. Morgan requires overhaul engines. Have arranged with form. to have the work carried out independently which to provide two men sent to work in the work — There have though made up in Carpenters shop + Iron out by thinkers by D.A.D.M.S	
			Lieut. Galloway ordered to L.H.O. Troops for duty.	SC
	17/12		Lieut. 10.19. Hutchinson arrived for duty — duty C.B. + 16.9. Sh/14. 2/5	SD
	18/12		No remarks.	
	19/12		Visited 11.0¹ 11.0², 11.0² 2/110² 2 Infantry Brigades also 155² Fd EA.4 5 Reg R.H.of	
	20/12		Received further issue of motorcars from 5 Leather jerkins all mobs now complete	200
	21/12		Strictly Conference of Quartermasters of 60 hr Supts - to discuss reserve Reserve 12" issue of Table Lehnds.	500
				500

T2134. Wt. W708—776. 500000. 4/15. Sir J. C. & S.

WAR DIARY
or
INTELLIGENCE SUMMARY.

(Erase heading not required.)

Army Form C. 2118.

Place	Date	Hour	Summary of Events and Information	Remarks and references to Appendices
Pres.	23/12		No remarks	
	24/12		Visited 119th Brigade Hd Qrs. Also Divn Troops Mobile Workshop Ford	
	25/12		No remarks	
	26/12		Visited 110th Brigade Hd Qrs; also Refilling Point	W.T.F
	27/12		Major Greaves arrived at R.D.S.O.S. This Army attacks & inspects K Divisional Workshops	W.T.F
	28/12		Visited Hd Qrs Division & reviewed 6 P.B.I. brevets & for advance for purpose of	W.T.F 05/4
			being told, acceptly to instructions	W.T.F
			At Divary HQ before lunch made purchase of articles up to £9. 15. 7½	W.T.F
	29/12		required by Brigade & to 1/12 Brigade	W.T.F 10.T.F
	30/12		Visited 112 Brigade Hd Qrs	W.T.F
			Visited 110 Brigade Hd Qrs; also 13 & 14 Ordnance Workshops, Lowestrie	W.T.F
	31/12		No remarks	Air'n W.T.F

DADOS
37th Division

War Diary for
month of
January 1916.

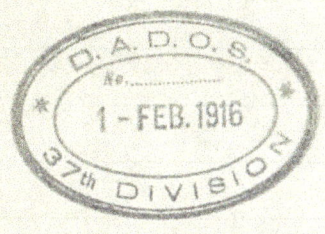

W. D. Harbinson Lieut
DADOS

WAR DIARY
or
INTELLIGENCE SUMMARY.
(Erase heading not required.)

Army Form C. 2118.

Instructions regarding War Diaries and Intelligence Summaries are contained in F. S. Regs., Part II. and the Staff Manual respectively. Title pages will be prepared in manuscript.

Place	Date	Hour	Summary of Events and Information	Remarks and references to Appendices
	1916			
Pas	1/1		Received consignment of 1896 boots from Mjr L. Drinkwater to be distributed by A.A. + Q.m.g. I viz 1000 pairs to 110th Infantry Brigade + 896 prs to 111th Infantry Brigade. Wrote S.D.V.S., 3rd Army	6.S.H. 6.S.H. 6.S.H.
"	2/1		The Director of Ordnance Services - General Parsons - accompanied by Major A.D.H. Baker visits the Ordnance Depot + inspects the workshops.	6.S.H.
"	3/1		Capt Collison left to take up his duties as D.A.D.O.S. 55th Division	6.S.H.
"	4/1		In compliance with arrangements made by H. General Staff M.L. Division conducted a number of Officers selected from various sub M.L. Divisions through M.L. workshops + explabts in detail the methods of + system adopted. Received the workshops + explabts in detail the methods of + system adopted.	11.S.H. 11.S.H.
"	5/1		Took car + travellers + forcespie t.filth to heavy mobile workshop at Beauval, of same went to Doullens + made some local purchases	11.S.H.
"	6/1		Visited Hqrs 1st + 2nd 110 + 111 Infantry Brigades + made enquiries as to their requirements. Received no complaints whatever. Lofor John Fitzroy May 5 worked 11.S.H.	11.S.H. 6.S.H.
"	7/1		Firstly Telegraph visits the parkland at Bondicourt Went to divily further of purchase of purchasing material urgently required in 11.S.H. 11. Division workshops	6.S.H. 6.S.H.

WAR DIARY
or
INTELLIGENCE SUMMARY.
(Erase heading not required.)

Army Form C. 2118.

Place	Date	Hour	Summary of Events and Information	Remarks and references to Appendices
Pos	8/1		Went to Army Printing works at Beauval & afterwards saw Col. 4th	4th
"			Baker at the office of D.D.O.S. 3rd Army in respect of question of demands 3rd Army
"			for clothing	4th
"	9/1		No remarks	4th
"	10/1		Visited A.D.O.S. VII Corps at Moreuil & discussed with him several questions 4th
"			concerning the internal administration of the Division. He draws attention 4th
"			to the demands made by units in regard to further stocks of Caps & during the 4th
"			the last few months of 1915 represented views that for the future a reduction 4th
"			should be made to the same of these to the articles of clothing.
"			Calls at the office of O.O. VII Corps Troops at Moreuil & these there wheels 4th
"			attaching hooks have since been made for trade with the Division.
"	11/1		No remarks	4th
"	12/1			4th
"	13/1		Visits the Headquarters of the 110th, 111th, & 112th Infantry Brigades, takes the HQ Bgd 4th
"			of 2nd Divn. Batt. Bomb. Reg't. Impresses upon Staff Captains the desirability of 4th
"			obtaining minor repairs to fur Boots carried out by units	4th
"	14/1		Attends at Rainlaw at H.M. Court & in afternoon on parade at a lecture at 4th
"			Hdqrs VIII Corps on the Orwich who reminds the remains the prevent the Batt. of boots 4th

Army Form C. 2118.

WAR DIARY
or
INTELLIGENCE SUMMARY.
(Erase heading not required.)

Instructions regarding War Diaries and Intelligence Summaries are contained in F.S. Regs., Part II. and the Staff Manual respectively. Title pages will be prepared in manuscript.

Place	Date	Hour	Summary of Events and Information	Remarks and references to Appendices
Pas	15/1		Went to Amiens though one Super's suit by overcoat with H.Q. Parcel	
"	16/1		No remarks	W.D.H
"	17/1		Called at M.H.Qrs. of M. 111th Brigade. Made arrangements at Ordnance Dump for a hurried through inspection of all clothing returned as unserviceable from units	W.D.H
"	18/1		Called at M.H.Qrs. of M. 110th Brigade re. M. Staff Capt. regarding M demands for spare parts of Lewis Machine Guns. Visited Mine is & Workshops. In afternoon compared M.T. Workshop Lifeaids & Quartermasters & Quartermasters Serjts. attn. defects, work checked. Points as to the necessity of exercising great vigilance with a view to reducing the demands of M. Division for Clothing & other expendable stores.	W.D.H
"	19/1		Called at M. office of O.O. M.Corps Troops at Moreuil to collect some Lamps electric signals &, went from there D.M. Heavy Mobile Workshops at Beauval to get one Limbers that were being repaired & returned by Smellier store Limbers at any rate, repaired by M.H.Qrs. M.M. Corps &c	W.D.H
"	20/1		Major Heavey, assistant to D.D.O.S., Third Army visited Pas & inspected Ordnance Stores, Workshops &c	W.D.H

WAR DIARY or INTELLIGENCE SUMMARY

Army Form C. 2118.

Place	Date	Hour	Summary of Events and Information	Remarks and references to Appendices
Pas	21/1		Went to the Hd. Qrs. of the 110, 111 & 112 Inf. Bdes. and arrangements for representatives of the various units & others of their respective Brigades Hd. Qrs. to receive instruction from a specialist with regard to form lights.	W.I.H.
"	22/1		Visits Amiens & returned to lamp which was conveyed from the Chemin de fer du Nord for the purpose of experiments by the O.C. Hd. Qrs. Signal 37th Div. Made some purchases for the Div. workshops and returned by the Div. workshops, Beauval, & collected final legible fluid lights which were left there for additional supply.	W.I.H.
"	23/1		Calls at Marieux to see A.D.V.S. III Div. & gave them supply of lantern test feeding for use with Division	W.I.H.
"	24/1		Col. Warwick A.D.V.S. III Corps called at the Ordnance Office & received	A.I.H.
"	25/1		The took dealing with bulk issues. Collected the lamps electric signalling to O.O. 7th Corps Troops, Moreuise, representing calls at the Hd. Qrs. of the 111th Infantry Bde and made arrangements for the supply of certain stores required for the Bombing School which is about to be opened.	W.I.H.
"	26/1		Left some articles for repair at Heavy Mobile workshops, Beauval, and (inc) issues for workshops and (inc) issues to Amiens. Made and went to Amiens for workshops	W.I.H.

WAR DIARY
or
INTELLIGENCE SUMMARY.

Army Form C. 2118.

Place	Date	Hour	Summary of Events and Information	Remarks and references to Appendices
Pao	27/1		Went to Snellows in aeroplane with instructions for A.D.T., III Corps., who took delivery of 5000 "P" tubes which he holds full Divisional reserve. There are as it apparents no orders father inside behind.	W.D.H
"	28/1		No remarks	
"	29/1		Received notification that a Sqn. detached 7th Indian Cavalry Corps. was to attached to this Division. That they would receive their Ordnance supplies from —	W.D.H
"	30/1		Twenty five additional Lewis Guns arrived out of a total of fifty, which have been demanded in accordance with instructions from Thirdarmy, have come to hand; also 100 rails for anipers of were demanded in accordance with D.D.O. Received instructions from "Q" to once more proceed with the making of barricades & Divisional workshops.	W.D.H
"	28/31/1		Bear Colonel Stanton. Barrett D.D.O., Third Army visited Pao & inspected the Divisional workshops.	W.D.H

W. D. Hoskinson Lieut.
D.O.D.U.S. 37 Div.

War Diary
for
February, 1916.

37th Div
29-2-16.

W. D. Harbinson Lieut
DADOS

WAR DIARY
or
INTELLIGENCE SUMMARY
(Erase heading not required.)

Army Form C. 2118.

Place	Date	Hour	Summary of Events and Information	Remarks and references to Appendices
Pas	1916 Feb 1st		Our Tirl conference of Divisional motor Transport serving for M purpose of opening a checking of vehicles. Col. Warwick A.D.S.T. Explained to workshop "some of M Workshops	W.D.H.
"	2		Visited niellow tales went to Smelins & by & Amelens came train for workshop	W.D.H.
"	3		No remarks	W.D.H.
"	4		Went to Amiens Purchased amongst Stn things for M men & moved for M Salvage Co. These items to be made up with Divisional Workshops	W.D.H.
"	5		Issued to N, III Infantry Bde. 3200 smoke helmets (P tube) to replace those which were worn during Ny recent gas scare. This number together with 2700 already issued comes to 110 % + 112 % Infy Bdes. + 187 the supplies to the Artillery will bring the total issued in these area to a little over Then 6000.	W.D.H.
"	6		Went to Railhead see 8 arrival of four 4.7 guns for 9" heavy battery Subaguez car I.O.M. at VII Corps Workshops & charges for repair of Tailboards for 50 "12 field Ambulance	W.D.H.

Army Form C. 2118.

WAR DIARY
or
INTELLIGENCE SUMMARY.
(Erase heading not required.)

Instructions regarding War Diaries and Intelligence Summaries are contained in F. S. Regs., Part II. and the Staff Manual respectively. Title pages will be prepared in manuscript.

Place	Date	Hour	Summary of Events and Information	Remarks and references to Appendices
Pas	Feb 7	1916	Went to railhead in order to arrange for the despatch of the Base of men 4.7 guns which were being returned by a the Heavy Bty. Subsequently went to their Army Workshops, Beauval, Werkletts cistern which what been left here for repair	W.D.H.
"	8		Received orders from A.D.O.S. that a number of tent fitters had been withdrawn from units of the Division & orders were to put tent to Corps. Saw various units of various units & made all necessary arrangements.	A.D.H.
"	9		Went to Bovincourt to try & try & find supplies for this Sept orders a "dump" for the stores when the OC contemplates charge of Division Ad Ors that village is in fine effect to.	W.D.H.
"	10		Took orders for repair to the heavy workshops, Beauval, to form while the D.R.O.S. Third Army, showed the question of the ordnance the Divisional workshops in view of the proposed removal of Divisional Hd Ors to Bavincourt.	W.D.H.
"	11		No remarks	
"	12		Went to Bavincourt to what of Sir Alger. are the charged relates to buildings for Ordnance workshops & dumps	A.D.H.

WAR DIARY
or
INTELLIGENCE SUMMARY.
(Erase heading not required.)

Army Form C. 2118.

Instructions regarding War Diaries and Intelligence Summaries are contained in F. S. Regs., Part II. and the Staff Manual respectively. Title pages will be prepared in manuscript.

Place	Date	Hour	Summary of Events and Information	Remarks and references to Appendices
Poo	Feb 13		Went to Workshops III Corps at Souastre & arranged with O.M. Scarlett to draw covers of the intercepts with him. Buses wheels are still unconverted	T.1.40H
"	14		No remarks	
	15		Col Lawrie A.D.O.S. III Corps called. Informed him of M arrangements made at M new H.Q. Ors., Bavincourt, for carrying on M Divisional Workshops & pressed for endenting M Ordnance Services of M Division	6.5H 0.5H
	16		Went to Bavincourt with M Chief Clerk, M Armourer, in feet to M Ordnance. Decided to/behind M noms full Divisional Workshops	W.S.H.
	17		Went to Amiens tonight — one lamp burning for M bus & Ily Decorator for 66 D.	
	18		Visited H.Q. Or. 111th Infantry Bde; also H.Q. Or. 10th Batt Royal Fusiliers & discussed with O.C. & Quartermaster M best means of reducing the demand for boots by M unit. Arranged to return to M latter M bulk of the twelvemonth lot of M Divisional Shoemaker shop.	W.S.H.
	19		Transferred M Divisional Reserve of socks marking M Div reserve D.R. Infy helmets to new Gen H.Q. Ors. at Bavincourt. Visits H.Q. Ors. of 110 & 112 Infantry Brigades.	

Army Form C. 2118.

WAR DIARY
or
INTELLIGENCE SUMMARY.
(Erase heading not required.)

Instructions regarding War Diaries and Intelligence Summaries are contained in F. S. Regs., Part II. and the Staff Manual respectively. Title pages will be prepared in manuscript.

Place	Date	Hour	Summary of Events and Information	Remarks and references to Appendices
Pos	Jul 20		Removed ammonal fixtures to Bouvancourt where spare holes drilled ready to receive it. Ordnance staff left to join us for our Hd. Qrs.	O.C. W.S.H.
Bouvancourt	21		left Pos Chu morning & spent day in improving our camp & HQrs. workshops & enabling members of the unit to settle in their quarters	W.S.H.
"	22		Visits in conformity with C.C., Divne. A.A. & Q.M.G. this Sir., VII Corps workshops. Arrange for a systematic overhaul of the Lewis machine guns of Divn. & left an armourer with R.O.M. to assist his armourer in firing immediate effect of this project	W.S.H.
"	23		At Amiens. Bought material for M workshop. Travel expenses from M sir. at store. M. J. Wells & co runs for workshop has almost run out. Collects a considerable strength to M had to been sent by motor to Beure	saddles W.S.H. W.S.H. Beure
"	24		to regiment instead of through the Divisions	
"	25		No Remarks	W.H.
"	26		Passed the day at Bouvancourt supervising work. In accordance with instructions detailed as "P.H." title letters for HQ Bouve at the rate of one for W.S.H. each officer train with Divisions	

T2134. Wt. W708-776. 500000. 4/15. Sir J. C. & S.

Place	Date	Hour	Summary of Events and Information	Remarks and references to Appendices
Barancourt	Feb 27		Lewis new machine guns (Lewis pattern) at M. not of 2 per battalion. The increase brings the number of Lewis guns with Bn. in up to one per battalion.	W.S.H
	28		Great difficulty in remounting Ordnance stores from railhead owing to very bad possibility in not m transport. Train's railheads & promise were changed for the purpose.	W.S.H
"	29		Trailer Railers in company with Capt Airey D.A.Q.M.G. arranged at 11 round of detail stores at 9 PM 195 boxes of "P.H." Tube Helmets, etc. experiencing great difficulty to keep them distributed to units - owing to the continuance of M restrictions on traffic & emergence of M trains.	

C. 2118

D.A.D.O.S.
37th Division.
(Capt. W. D. Harbinson).

War Diary for
March 1916.

37 Div
2.4.16.

WAR DIARY or INTELLIGENCE SUMMARY

Army Form C. 2118.

(Erase heading not required.)

Place	Date	Hour	Summary of Events and Information	Remarks and references to Appendices
Barisnent	April 1st		Visits Raillers & 57th stores clearing by lorry - Transport stores 57th units by same means. Subsequently went to 57th Pets School at this Am & H.O. Ord. Other cyls of packing belonging to salon brethren etc. Deposits some articles at this thing. Ingrely ordered to come which lately required 57 Div. Took various articles which had arrived on vidat 57th Division School of Instruction, Lockerne	
	2			W.S.H.
	3		No Remarks	6.7H
	4		Three Brigade Machine Gun Companies - 110th, 111th & 112th - arrived for the attached 57th Division. Sent to Pas to O.O. VIII Corps troops for General Shapes which have been issued with Mauthart & ADVS VIII Corps. Most unfor to be returned to Corps out of 57th twenty five still due 57th Division in addty they are received	
	5		In Company with Col. Bowen A.A. & Q.M.G. 57th Div. I visits R Three brigade machine gun companies which have just come from England. I meet one they reports that they were fully equipped except for a few stones for their Lindele Bowr. Indely 68H repts VIII Corps Ordnance Workshops at Savelly + arranges for their lever + repair of the	W.S.H
	6		Visits VIII Corps Ordnance 111 Sd Bde Rifle mortars.	W.S.H

Army Form C. 2118.

WAR DIARY
or
INTELLIGENCE SUMMARY.
(Erase heading not required.)

Instructions regarding War Diaries and Intelligence Summaries are contained in F. S. Regs., Part II. and the Staff Manual respectively. Title pages will be prepared in manuscript.

Place	Date	Hour	Summary of Events and Information	Remarks and references to Appendices
Barracont	June 7		No remarks	A.S.H.
	8		Conference of Quartermasters this month. Inspected the two tube of A.S. Divisional Theatre. Col. Avery two attached by Col. Bourne A.A. & Q.M.G. of Division. Also inspected for same all the records & returns of Army.	A.S.H.
	9		Attended a conference of D.A.D's of III Corps Divisions held by Col. Warwick A.D.O.S. at III R. Corps H.Q. Ord.	A.S.H.
	10		Major Travers assistant E.M.S.D.O.S., Third Army, called & inspected the Stores & Workshops.	A.S.H.
	11		The first relay of men from units with M Division who attended at H.Q. Ord. in conference with A.D.O.S. 10.55 for a three days' course of instruction at the Armourers' Shop having completed their course returned to their units; second batch gone by a similar course duly reported. Made some purchases at Amiens for M Div. Shops, etc. Col. Kelly, R.A. & Q.M.G. of 4 R.Div visits "Army" Workshops, also Lieut Kirkby D.A.D.O.S. of same Div.	A.S.H.
	12 p.m.			A.S.H.
	13		No remarks	A.S.H.

Army Form C. 2118.

WAR DIARY
or
INTELLIGENCE SUMMARY.
(Erase heading not required.)

Place	Date	Hour	Summary of Events and Information	Remarks and references to Appendices
Duisans	March 14		Learned officially that it has been decided to transfer the A.O.D. of this Division. Believe in consequence of Division having into reserve. Orders noted by S.D.D. of 4 Divisn, L/C in Charge, L/L is take over Move offices etc. L/C to arrange to take over Move offices etc.	W. Dty 39 Div W. Dty
	15		Went to Lucheux, the new Div. A.O.D. to select an Ordnance Dump & arrange fleurs for offices, workshops &c	W. Dty
	16		Col. Warwick A.D.O.S. VII Corps came to discuss various questions regarding administration. In the evg. Lieut. VII Corps Workshops & arranged with Lieut Brown O.C.M. for an inspection of transport & the vehicles of the Division	W. Dty
	17		Again at Lucheux about suitable places for full workshops, some difficulties having arisen about places & programme of work. Anything better than at the shops required.	W. Dty
	18		Busy with papers	W. Dty
			Went to Lucheux with Major Lodor D.A.A. & Q.M.G. to try & arrange about workshop as owing to conflicting claims it was difficult to arrive at a definite decision. Ultimately allotted the places which had relation as suitable. Returned Ordnance Dump "stable" to Div. A.O. Lucheux.	W. Dty
	19			W. Dty

WAR DIARY or INTELLIGENCE SUMMARY

Army Form C. 2118.

Place	Date	Hour	Summary of Events and Information	Remarks and references to Appendices
Béthune	March 20		Left Bavincourt for Lucheux two occupied during the day in disposing of matters connected with the proper functioning of the Ordnance services in the new area.	
	21		Col. Warwick A.D.O.S. visited, checked & explained the arrangements that were made for the distribution of stores etc. the fuel approved.	D.D.H.
	22		Visited the heavy workshop, wheeled lorry made to I Divn & collected one a-vehicle that had been left for repair	D.D.H.
	23		Attended fortnightly conference at H.Q. Office of A.D.O.S. VII Corps. Discussed P.A.D. & M.T. units	D.D.H.
	24		In the afternoon accompanied Lt. Col. Browne D.D.O.S. on an inspection of M.T. transport of S.A.C. & other units	D.D.H.
	25		Saw the R.T.O. at Bergueneuse re incident concerning about trucks for returning to Paris. Units Clothing etc. still so run being sent back by R.T.O. Accompanied by Lieut Brown D.D.M. VII Corps inspected H.Q. transport whole to I Artillery Units	D.D.H.
	26		Wrote Soldbuch into Lt Col Kirkby S.D.O.S. II Division to take off the Ar.A. & 37 th Divn re "taking over" tents & the above whilst in being transferred from M.T. of	D.D.H.

WAR DIARY
or
INTELLIGENCE SUMMARY

Army Form C. 2118.

Place	Date	Hour	Summary of Events and Information	Remarks and references to Appendices
Lucknow	27th		Capt Hartmann proceeded to England on leave. Capt Imfreedy & Lt. on duties proceed to Lucknow.	
"	28th		No 3 Supply Train arrives at Mhow & is retained to 29 Reserve & ammunition.	
"	29th		No remark.	
"	30th		Arrangements made with Senior Army Medical to repair of Vehicles with "Telegraphic Code".	
"	31st		No remark.	

A.F. Keeling Capt
L & A.D.S.
27 Division

DADOS
37 Vol 8

War Diary
for
April - 1916.

37th Div
2. 5. 16

W. D. Hodkinson
Captain
~~DADOS~~

Army Form C. 2118.

WAR DIARY
or
INTELLIGENCE SUMMARY
(Erase heading not required.)

Instructions regarding War Diaries and Intelligence Summaries are contained in F. S. Regs., Part II. and the Staff Manual respectively. Title pages will be prepared in manuscript.

Place	Date	Hour	Summary of Events and Information	Remarks and references to Appendices
Lucheux	1916 April 1st		Orders received for the return of "field" clothing.	
"	2nd		No remark	
"	3rd		No remarks	
"	4		No remarks	
"	5		Col. Goodhew - Barrett. D.D.D. III Army, calls & inspects workshops. He	
"	6		expressed satisfaction with what he saw.	O.D.H.
"	7		No remarks	O.D.H.
"	8		Col. Warwick A.D.O.S. III Corps, calls & inspects R stores.	O.D.H.
"	9		In conformity with arrangements into clothing being returned to units	O.D.H.
"	10		best to III Corps workshops to convention with carrying out of return to	O.D.H.
"	11		vehicles with M.T. Division	O.D.H.
"	12		No remarks	
"	13		Spent the day in office running Div. workshops, stores &c	U.D.H.
			Went to Amiens with M.A.A. & D.M. of SR. Div. to purchase a number of wheels	W.D.H.
			for Div. Arts & School	W.D.H.
			No remarks	W.D.H.

WAR DIARY
or
INTELLIGENCE SUMMARY.
(Erase heading not required.)

Army Form C. 2118.

Place	Date	Hour	Summary of Events and Information	Remarks and references to Appendices
Lucheux	1916 April 14		Winter clothing being despatched to Paris for repair &c. Have arranged for two Div. Armourers attg. a course of instruction in Optical sights at Corps School	W.D.H
"	15		Visited Div. Baths at Pas & inspected clothing prior to its being sent to M Base	W.D.H
"	16		No remarks	W.D.H
"	17		Col. Warwick A.D.O.S. VII Corps, came & discussed several matters having on administration	W.D.H
"	18		Attended in company with Capt. Airey, S.A.O.M.S., & experience of Quartermasters of M 110th & 118th Bgde. cells. Full jupon clothing included.	W.D.H
"	19		Conference of Quartermasters at 9 A.M. 112 M Bde at Div. H.Qrs	W.D.H
"	20		Attended Conference M Stores & A.D.O.S. VII Corps at Pas.	W.D.H
"	21		Col. Warwick, A.D.O.S. VII Corps, called & looked through some of M books.	W.D.H
"	22		Went to Amiens & brought some articles that were urgently required relating a small part for one of M. Singer machines with Div. workshops	W.D.H
"	23		No remarks	W.D.H
"	24		Col. Warwick, A.D.O.S. VII Corps, called & examined M books recording entertaining of clearance	W.D.H

WAR DIARY
or
INTELLIGENCE SUMMARY.
(Erase heading not required.)

Army Form C. 2118.

Place	Date 1916	Hour	Summary of Events and Information	Remarks and references to Appendices
Lahowr	April 25		Instd workshops I.O.M III Corps at Sault: in connection with M repairs vehicles for units within Div; also delivered spare parts to ascertain [?]	
"	26		Instruction to O.C. VIII Corps Troops at Pas. No remarks	a.S.H
"	27		Col. Warwick A.D.O.S. III Corps called + discussed matters connected with M workshop & depot	W.S.H
"	28		Learnt that the Division is about to return the position in the line which it formerly held	W.S.H
"	29		I. interference in charge of Div. A.O.S. arranges for all for the withdrawal from tatoye VIII next St Marie M Kaple	W.S.H
"	30		Lieut Kirk D.A.D.O.S. III Division came in the afternoon to seek workshops. Officers that he will take over when III Division come into this area	W.S.H

W. D. Harkness
Capt.

DADOS 37th D
Vol 9

C-2118

D.A.D.O.S.
1 - JUN. 1916
37th DIVISION

War Diary
for
May. 1916

37th Div
1-6-16

W. D. Hobson
Capt
DADOS.

WAR DIARY
or
INTELLIGENCE SUMMARY.
(Erase heading not required.)

Army Form C. 2118.

Place	Date	Hour	Summary of Events and Information	Remarks and references to Appendices
Lucheux	1916 May 1		Went to III Corps workshops to arrange C.R.E. for repairs of vehicles & afterwards visited Heavy Mobile Workshop at Prevent & place-action at Rebecq.	
			Week ending 8th of May. Division	W.D.H.
	2		Col. Maclean & Barrett, D.D.V.S. III Army called, made enquiries as	W.D.H.
			return of works clothing. Also reports the doverhills of an Army-Staff Serjt.	
			being attached travel troops de Marche for C.S. with rank of acting Sergeant with	W.D.H.
	3		Left Lucheux for Bouval & have all day in stabling & billets to	
			Attacks employed at all Offices at D.H.Q. III Corps	W.D.H.
Bouval	4			
	5		Col. Barrett, A.D.V.S. III Corps, called. Spent all day arranging things generally	
			at new H.Q.rs.	W.D.H.
	6		Col. Barrett, A.D.V.S. III Corps, called. Decided that School called the	
			village Vets in certain areas to certain areas should the Division recover	
			vacated.	W.D.H.
	7		No remarks	W.D.H.
	8		Visited certain districts in the area just quitted by III Division arranged to collect	
			the village stores & bring them to the Group War at Bouval	W.D.H.

Army Form C. 2118.

WAR DIARY
or
INTELLIGENCE SUMMARY.
(Erase heading not required.)

Instructions regarding War Diaries and Intelligence Summaries are contained in F. S. Regs., Part II. and the Staff Manual respectively. Title pages will be prepared in manuscript.

Place	Date	Hour	Summary of Events and Information	Remarks and references to Appendices
Beaurevoir Aveluy	9 May 1916		Collected a quantity of village stores — being actively supplied by the Dept for shelves. Le Touret & the 9th began above the shelter left by M. Div. Fleet quitted the area.	
	10		Went to Amiens for the purpose of procuring some shells urgently required at Div. W.S.A. workshop	W.S.A.
	11		No remarks	W.S.A.
	12		Col Warwick OCAO A.D.O.S. VIII Corps called & inspected stores &c	W.S.A.
	13		Major Bailey Bom of M Staff M. Financial Adviser visited the office & dept workshops. Reported thoroughly in favor. He examined the method of checking issues with & defrayed all M. contents etc held, and referred himself satisfied with	W.S.A.
	14		Col Thornton - Barrett, B.D.O.S., VIII Army, came & looked through inspected. Q III "Hole" & inspected workshops & store.	W.S.A.
	15		Made some enclosures at Pondelon for Div. H.Q. Ors.	W.S.A.
	16		Received first consignment of 4 SMO satchels taken over the scheme for broke wheels of	W.S.A.
	17		No remarks	W.S.A.
	18		Spent day supervising workshops & administration of M. office generally	W.S.A.

WAR DIARY
or
INTELLIGENCE SUMMARY.
(Erase heading not required.)

Army Form C. 2118.

Place	Date	Hour	Summary of Events and Information	Remarks and references to Appendices
Beaurains	May 1916			
	19		No remarks	W.D.T.
"	20		Received notification for III Army that number of heavy guns for both workshops to supply & despatch is to be 4-5 % above Establishment according. Made arrangements at Doullens for divisional workshops	
				C.D.T.
	21		Went to Ordnance Heavy workshop, Prevent, re arranges for own supply steals. The supplies of this Division	C.D.T. T.H.B.S.
	22		Leaving for Boulogne tomorrow I am to take part with proceedings of a Court Martial on next front of M accused.	S.D.T. T.H.B.S.
"	23		No remarks	S.D.T. T.H.B.S.
" "	24		Capt. Shrubb took over duties of Ordnance officer during Capt. Harbison's absence at Boulogne.	C.D.T.
	25		No remarks	
" "	26		No remarks	C.D.T.
	27		No remarks	C.D.T.
	28		Returned from Boulogne where I was taking part as next field's " " Court Martial proceedings.	C.D.T.
	29			C.D.T.

Army Form C. 2118.

WAR DIARY
or
INTELLIGENCE SUMMARY.
(Erase heading not required.)

Instructions regarding War Diaries and Intelligence Summaries are contained in F. S. Regs., Part II. and the Staff Manual respectively. Title pages will be prepared in manuscript.

Place	Date	Hour	Summary of Events and Information	Remarks and references to Appendices
Bavincourt	12	19h		
	29		Lieut R. J. W. Sponders, A.D.B. reports for instruction in W. duties of Staff of a Division.	U.S.H.
	30		Attended conference of D. Directors re 9 Division at Div HdQrs also all units were checked	U.S.H.
	31		In company with AA & QMG made a tour through W Divisional area, calling amongst the places, at Hd Qrs 7th 111th & 112th Inf Brigades	U.S.H.

U.S.Harbinson Capt
D.A.D.O.S 37 Div

C. 2118.

DADOS
37th Division

War Diary for
June 1916

37th Div
2.VII.16

W. S. Harkinson
Capt.
DADOS.

Army Form C. 2118.

WAR DIARY
or
INTELLIGENCE SUMMARY.
(Erase heading not required.)

Instructions regarding War Diaries and Intelligence Summaries are contained in F. S. Regs., Part II. and the Staff Manual respectively. Title pages will be prepared in manuscript.

Place	Date	Hour	Summary of Events and Information	Remarks and references to Appendices
Barisend	June 1916			
	1		Spent the day attending to the routine work of Ordnance and inspection other Division Dr + also to inspection of R Div. workshops	G. S.H
	2		Col Warwick A.D.O.S. VIII Corps, called + we discussed various questions affecting Division independently - Conference with Fleet Spiller 8 wrotes 37 R Dw Railhead as R.R.O.O	G. S.H
	3		Received from the Base Dt a consignment of 2172 "P.H.J." helmets for distribution to Div. according to scale laid down by 3rd Army.	G. S.H
	4		No remarks	G. S.H
	5		Col Warrick A.D.O.S., VIII Corps called, went to Doullens for R purposes	G. S.H
	6		R purchasing returns for Divisional workshops	
	7		Gen R forward inspection of am details of units for Armed Posts with Div. area for R purposes meaning the condition of their uniform to to inspect pistol rebels leather and line Gr	G. S.H
			R afternoon made one inclose to Amiens	
	8		Attended conference at the A.D.O.S. Office. Explained new system of book keeping for bulk demands. Also Warwick called in the afternoon + ordered certain stores to be sent to the Base	West
	9		Sent a quantity of Equipment + rifles to Histone on withdrawal of A.D.O.S. VII Corps.	Mr. S

Army Form C. 2118.

WAR DIARY
or
INTELLIGENCE SUMMARY.
(Erase heading not required.)

Instructions regarding War Diaries and Intelligence Summaries are contained in F.S. Regs., Part II. and the Staff Manual respectively. Title pages will be prepared in manuscript.

Place	Date	Hour	Summary of Events and Information	Remarks and references to Appendices
Hin cond	10/6/16		Col. Warwick called. Discussed question of disinfection & washing of unserviceable underclothing & for despatch to Base. Instructed him to see AAGQMG. who should put up a case if there are difficulties in the way of getting washing done here. Drawing stores from Mendicourt - arrangements were plaeed by storemen. AHQRMS loaned some kit stores; spoke with regard to installing & re-training plant within his Divisions. 48 No.7 Drab Sights received from his Base.	MS
	11/6/16		Railhead changed to Doullens as Mendicourt is not very convenient.	
	12/6/16		Went to Doullens to see Hardwood(?) articles by local purchase	12/5
	13 June		Col. Warrick visited Th Stan & workshops & examined books & records	O.S.H.
	14 "		No remarks	O.S.H.
	15 "		Quiet M day in Office & inspected M.O. Div. Workshops	W.S.H.
	16 "		Received Box Consignment of Box Respirators	O.S.H.
	17 "		Made arrangements for M distribution of Box Respirators according to send arr. & emit out distribution according M	O.S.H.
	18		Various Box Respirators & Box Requisites Sent Mules ASD re to been receiving instruction with dates for Div Ordnance Officers returned to Havre	W.S.H.

T.2134. Wt. W708-776. 500000. 4/16. Sir J. C. & S.

Army Form C. 2118.

WAR DIARY
or
INTELLIGENCE SUMMARY.
(Erase heading not required.)

Instructions regarding War Diaries and Intelligence Summaries are contained in F.S. Regs., Part II. and the Staff Manual respectively. Title pages will be prepared in manuscript.

Place	Date	Hour	Summary of Events and Information	Remarks and references to Appendices
Bertincourt	June 19	1916	No remarks	
	20		Called at H.Q. Heavy Artillery Group (48th) with reference to 4 guns (60 pr) which he had arrived. Selected "dump" at Lebut for Battery required to be in a position on attack	C. SA
	21		Went to Amiens for M. before I wheeling colour wheels supports required by the Division	C. SA
	22		No remarks	C. SA
	23		Went to H.Q. R.A. & called upon D.D.O.S. III Army.	C. SA
	24		Spent the day in making preparations for offensive operations	C. SA
	25		No remarks	O. SA
	26		Went to Amiens & made certain purchases in accordance with instructions received of "Q" branch	C. SA
	27		In conference with H.Q. A.A. & Q.M.G. visited certain areas with H. Dineen	C. SA
	28		Quiet day. Inspecting routine work at my office	C. SA
	29		Spent morning at Office & Workshops. In the afternoon made some further allocations	C. SA
	30		Kept Proof M.U. Div. Ammn Column & Div. Artillery School, 46 field ambulance	C. SA
			J.O. M'Crackston R (III Corps) HC	W.S.A

Army Form C. 2118.

WAR DIARY
or
INTELLIGENCE SUMMARY.
(Erase heading not required.)

Instructions regarding War Diaries and Intelligence Summaries are contained in F. S. Regs., Part II. and the Staff Manual respectively. Title pages will be prepared in manuscript.

Place	Date	Hour	Summary of Events and Information	Remarks and references to Appendices
Bainicourt	July 1	1916	Went to Toeuvres to collect kit from to myself, reported & arrange for a number to establish stores for Div team. In afternoon went through Div. area & called at H.Q. of 17 of 1st three infantry brigades. W. B. Robinson Capt.	

37/ Levy

DADOS 37 Div
VOL II

C 2118

War Diary
of
DADOS. 37d Div
for
July 1916

W. D. Harbinson
Capt
DADOS

37 Div
1-viii-16

Army Form C. 2118.

WAR DIARY
or
INTELLIGENCE SUMMARY.
(Erase heading not required.)

Instructions regarding War Diaries and Intelligence Summaries are contained in F. S. Regs., Part II. and the Staff Manual respectively. Title pages will be prepared in manuscript.

Place	Date	Hour	Summary of Events and Information	Remarks and references to Appendices
Beaurevoir	9.9.27	1916	1 Sent to Advance Intel HQ Front, to collect orders regarding reports of trains	
			2 visits H.A. O/c of M 110, 111, 112 & 112 Inf. Bdes.	6. S.H.
			3 Made preliminary arrangements w/ new H.Q. O/c J. Division moving to the area	4. S.H.
Pos			4 visits Pos where new H.Q. O/c J. Division will be situated & have an office re S.R.H.	
			Moved to Pos along with Div'l HQ O/c. Advance Pos at present about three kilometres distant from Pos. The arrangement is inconvenient but we must along to Corps Orders	
			5 Went to Advance Posts during the morning & afternoon work there	4. S.H.
			6 afternoon visits A.P.O's III Corps	6. S.H.
			7 Spent part of the day at Pos and the other part of the day at the "Dump" at four cross roads	4. S.H.
			8 No remarks.	
			Called at M. HQ O/c of M 102 & 103 Inf Bdes which have fallen come about	
			Div to replace in Inf. Bdes detailed as joined with the Italian	U.S.H.
			Gofrapham which arrived at stores at four cross roads supervising work of	
			9 Sent out from B.L 63'D, 102, 370, 3 Dg. Bdes for the purpose of	4. S.H.
			10 ascertaining how they stood with rather of notices, & general etc.	

T.J.134. Wt. W708—776. 500000. 4/15. Sir J. C. & S.

Army Form C. 2118.

WAR DIARY
or
INTELLIGENCE SUMMARY.
(Erase heading not required.)

Instructions regarding War Diaries and Intelligence Summaries are contained in F. S. Regs., Part II. and the Staff Manual respectively. Title pages will be prepared in manuscript.

Place	Date	Hour	Summary of Events and Information	Remarks and references to Appendices
Pas	July 1916			
	11		No remarks	
	12		Spent ½ day between Pas & Frévent allotted gd & divnal work finished	4.S.H.
	13		Attended conference at H.Qrs. of A.D.D.S. III Corps	4.S.H.
	14		Closed Divn workshops rent Coy RE from 8 Divn wards information of Divn having III Corps area	4.S.H.
	15		The Divn left Pas & moved to Beauval. Billets at Beauval. Staff arrived at Beauval	4.S.H.
	16		Divn HQrs moves to Bonas	4.S.H.
	17		Divn HQrs remained at Bonas	4.S.H.
	18		Divn HQrs Staff at Bonas	4.S.H.
Beauval	19		Moved to Bonay with Ordnance dump & personnel. Thy being tt 37 gd	
			(Viellers it to Pigeons) & (Fiennes) RC Willers (remain Here distribut	
			storing from the castle	4.S.H.
	20		Installed at Bonay & commenced distributing stores to tt afternoon from a mark	
			to Divn H.Qrs at La Brute	4.S.H.
	21		Col Bonner A.D.& A.M.G. of the Divn calls & discussed questions of ce-fitting H Divn	4.S.H.
			with the best delay possible	4.S.H.
	22		No remarks	4.S.H.

Army Form C. 2118.

WAR DIARY
or
INTELLIGENCE SUMMARY.
(Erase heading not required.)

Place	Date	Hour	Summary of Events and Information	Remarks and references to Appendices
Fricourt	July 23	1916	Genl afternoon visits afforded H.Q. Div, Divl. Armoury. Visits H.Q. Div 37th Div. Artillery also H.Q. 102 Inf. Bde.	6. D.H.
"	24	"		4. D.H.
"	25	"	Attended conference D.Q. Quarters attd to 63 Inf. Bde where to gurshm	4. D.H.
"	26	"	Re equipping 112 Bde. Soon full come into. Visits to H.Q. Div at La Comte	6. D.H. 6. D.H.
"	27	"	Went to refitting point & the arrangement re the Staff Capt. & Q.Master 103 Fdes. also Settled Plan of refitting the units D.M. Bde.	2. M. Va. D.H.
"	28	"	Went to Corbie & turned in with II Corps & drew Stores for pers...	4 D.H.
"	29	"	intimately needed by the Divis. Went to G. Sir H.Q. Div at Canbtain Pratt & residents one store transpov from 47 H.Q. Div	6. D.H.
"	30	"	Visits H.Q. Div M. 102 & 103 Inf. Bdes. & also H.Q. 37 & 103 Machine Gun Cos. settles various Ordnance amounts with M. re fittis M. Infty with S.B.	
"	31	"	Visits various Centres in M Div area with refer to of available Salvage Ordnance Stores	W. D. H.

W.D. Hutchinson Capt.
DADOS. 37th Divs

37/DADOS/Vol 2

C. 2118

War Diary

for

August 1916

37th Div
31.8.16.

WAR DIARY
or
INTELLIGENCE SUMMARY.
(Erase heading not required.)

Army Form C. 2118.

Place	Date	Hour	Summary of Events and Information	Remarks and references to Appendices
Bruay	Aug 1	10ᵃ	Photos to artillery front with survey rect'd. Staff Capt. + O. of Arts to 102ⁿᵈ Inf Bde reported conference relative to rifting of TBOR. This is progressing satisfactorily	
"	" 2		Twenty field orders there S.O.s for upon import; subsequently went to Div. H.Q. Orr.	W. D.H.
"	" 3		No remarks	W. D.H.
"	" 4		Visits Div. HQ. Orr. subsequently went to II Corps (No. 8) switch instrob.	W. D.H.
"	" 5		Went to HQ Orr. & L. 63ʳᵈ Bde & subsequently to Divis. HQ. Orr.	W. D.H.
"	" 6		Sketch drawn and sent to Infantry & other units in Division	W. D.H.
"	" 7		Visits Div. H.Q. Orr. & other areas in Division	U. D.H.
"	" 8		Started day with visits & front round Obs. Div. HQrs. "dump" &c	W. D.H.
"	" 9		Passed whole hot of the day at "dump"; nothing unusual etc.; during th afternoon visits Div. HQ Orrs.	W. D.H.
"	" 10		No remarks approaching	O. D.H.
"	" 11		Visits units in connection with th transfer as Motion for th div. th. passes area	W. D.H.
"	" 12		Visits Div. HQ Orr. relative of the new area the occupied by the Div.	W. D.H.

WAR DIARY
or
INTELLIGENCE SUMMARY.
(Erase heading not required.)

Army Form C. 2118.

Place	Date	Hour	Summary of Events and Information	Remarks and references to Appendices
Bray	Aug 13	1916	I confer with Lt Col Browne, A.A. & Q.M.G. attached a conference of O.C.'s Hy Arty & medium fixed Mortar Batteries when Div Cr referred to completing their equipment.	L.D.H.
"	14		Visits Div H.Q. Order states Div Orr S.R. 103 & Hy Br 103 & Hy Artillery tommrw & orders no. 2971 magazines of Lewis guns & changes the number S.R. 9th Division to accordance with instructions of III Corps.	L.D.H.
"	15		No remarks	L.D.H.
"	16		Visits Nos 2 & No 8 Advance workshops (light) at Bruitz & Othain in connection with the guns taken over by the Div from 9 & 9 Div	L.D.H.
"	17		Visits III Army Heavy workshops at Fresnoy redirected & tons deposit	L.D.H.
"	18		New for repair before this Div left III Army area Cases of Ordnance workshop at Othain to arrange abt magazine of the Div; afterwards visits stores of Ord.D.O. III Div regarding rules & forms of magazines transferred this & accordance with instructions	L.D.H.
"	19 & 20th		No remarks (Capt Hardinson sick)	Morning trip
"	21st		Took over temporarily advance of 33rd Division as of A.D.O.S.	ADS
"	22nd		102nd & 103rd Brigades returned 34th Division & 112 & 113 Brigades returned this Division	ADS

WAR DIARY
or
INTELLIGENCE SUMMARY.
(Erase heading not required.)

Army Form C. 2118.

Place	Date	Hour	Summary of Events and Information	Remarks and references to Appendices
Fricourt	Aug 23	1916	Visited Brigade H.Qrs 112th & all units in Brigade to ascertain stores required. Set into Armourer Shop any guns etc for repair & complete Battalion with magazines.	PBD
"	24	"	Called at M. Horse. Visited G. Roche Stafford (Pioneers) at Villers au Bois re English recovery equipment.	PBD
"	25	"	Visited 3rd Derram Base St Maur (made arrangements for transfer of stores 102-103 Bdes to 111 & 112 Bdes). Visited Railhead & salvage Dump. Also 111 Brigade units to ascertain stores required.	PBD
"	26	"	Visited heavy motor Battery & M. Bus at Le Cauroi & found not stated of truck motors. Took parts on to No 1 Workshop at Oblain for reproduction. Called at DHQ.	PBD
"	27	"	No remarks	MD
"	28	"	Visited Oblain to take up Front Auxtn park which had been moved. Handed over to M. I.O. Bullitt at La Cante. Called as demanded those trucks.	PBD
"	29	"	In company of Col Ronne AD & DMA, OC Dis Rau & Captn Hyppolite SOA inspected 1st line transport of 63rd Brigade at Etru Candrie, Cauthau l'Abbé. Guy Harme & Chalon la Rose.	PBD
"	30	"	Visited Railhead & divisional Head Quarters.	PBD
"	31	"	No remarks. Visited DHQ & stated that M. & M. Bdes reinforcement machinists completed except for Lewis which had been delayed by trucks not arriving in Units at proper time.	PBD

3/9/16
PB Devereux
Lt A.R.D.O.
37th Division

37 Vol 13

C. 2118

DADOS 37th DS

War Diary
for
September 1916.

John H. Mocwats
Lieut
DADOS

WAR DIARY
or
INTELLIGENCE SUMMARY.
(Erase heading not required.)

Army Form C. 2118.

Place	Date	Hour	Summary of Events and Information	Remarks and references to Appendices
Bruay	Sept 1st/916		Visited units of 63rd Brigade, & 9 North Staff (Pioneers) to interview Commanders & Commanding Officers. Visited DHQ.	PJS
"	2nd	"	Further visited + 63rd Div troops re supplying him with transport. Lewis Guns & machinery visited Larn at Ollron (No 6 workshop) re schedule of 63rd Brigade on repairs. Also saw 111 Bde MGC at same.	PJSD
"	3rd	"	Lewis at Raichead & DHQ re further movements. Prepared for handing over to 2/Lieut Taylor % 6 Trench Appendices to Lewing for call up duties as sapper 63rd Tr. Division	PJSD
"	4th	"	Took over from Lieut Denison; engaged going through Office details etc; inspected workshops and billets	PJS
"	5th	"	Visited Railhead & entrain party re next own Storeroom; demanded 14000 blankets to complete to scale of 1 per man in accordance with 1st Army instructions; arranged with 111th Bde to workout at Lewis Gunn 13 R.B. and with 112th Bde. 2 Vickers Gun of 112th MG Coy 5 inst. Retained all rifles Bayonets & scabbards in Divnl Armourers Shop 1st Batt.	PJS
"	6th	"	Divis having taken own School at PERNES arranging to 2nd Cav Tailors Shop with a view to taking tailoring for the School; Sending 30 working parties to	PJS

Army Form C. 2118.

WAR DIARY
or
INTELLIGENCE SUMMARY.

(Erase heading not required.)

Instructions regarding War Diaries and Intelligence Summaries are contained in F. S. Regs., Part II. and the Staff Manual respectively. Title pages will be prepared in manuscript.

Place	Date	Hour	Summary of Events and Information	Remarks and references to Appendices
In the Field	1916 Sept			
	5th	6-11am	The school & also carrying three Officers instructed to 9 recruits from N Coys; inspecting workshops; informing 3rd Div that we had had nothing to do with reorganization from artillery; arranging with 13 R.F. to send for twenty kitchen ranges.	P.T.S.
"	7th	"	Visiting units of 112th Bde at BEUGIN & LACOMTE; also section of "B" echelon DAC, & arriving at HOUCHIN & explaining attitude of DAC now being relieved by 37th Div; subsequently visiting units of 63rd Bde at TREUILLERS (4 Coln) & at HERMIN (61 Sanit:!) meeting Staff Capt at former place. Discussing with Q.M.D.A.S. distribution of blankets of which 2000 are to be held in reserve; arranging to divide as far as possible equally Entrs. implements in the first instance.	P.T.S.
"	8th	"	The 80 shrinkly demanded by 137th Field Co had been ret'd; interview with D.A.D.O.S. 9th Div; ordering 12 dbl rifles to firing grounds & 7 divisions & despatching to school at PERNES, arranging to distribute 4500 Bombs from Brigde & 300 F.S. books; O stoves & RO 1724 did not appear to satisfaction in Divtl shops.	P.T.S.
"	9th 10		No remarks. Superintending the work of R. Office & workshops generally.	W.D.H. 6.D.A.

WAR DIARY
or
INTELLIGENCE SUMMARY.

Army Form C. 2118.

Place	Date	Hour	Summary of Events and Information	Remarks and references to Appendices
Beauval	Sept 11 1916		No remarks	
	12 "		I conferred with O.C. Div. Train & Dep. A.D.T. inspected the transport Deel units of M 112 Inf. Bde. This was found. Later on inspected Cooker. Lieut Manvell a O.P. arrived & assumed duties of D.A.D.O.S. of the Division.	W.S.H.
	13 "		Visited Dump, Workshops and went into the working of the Division with Capt Rawlinson who left for Hd Qtr 3rd Army in the afternoon. Visited "Q" Branch D.A.Q.	MATH.
	14 "		Called at Hd Qtr of 63, 111 & 112 Brigades on various matters. Visited No 2 & No 8 Travelling Cookers Workshops. Inspected shops and establishment arrangements, also Dumps. Discussed with "Q" question of distribution of Gum Boots & Strygers also the question of transport inspection.	Navy.

T2134. W¹. W708-776. 500000. 4/15. Sir J. C. & S.

WAR DIARY
or
INTELLIGENCE SUMMARY

Army Form C. 2118.

Place	Date	Hour	Summary of Events and Information	Remarks and references to Appendices
Bray	Sept 15 1916		Inspected shops. Called on O.C. Train re dressing inspection of transport & other matters affecting to wagons. A.D.O.S. called 12.15pm. 2.PM Rifle Inspection — all rifles found to be in good order & well kept. Visited the Dumps. To DHQ - chief about arrival of Artillery. Drafted orders for the greater efficiency of the shops & the greater cleanliness of the men's billets.	MH
	16th		To HdQrs at 123, 127 & 126 Bdes R.F.A. re gun deficiencies. — To HQ Div Arty re transfer & reorganization of the Artillery. Inspected Workshops & Dumps. Visited "Q". Informed by "Q" that this Division will take over from 63rd on the 20.	
	17th		Arrangements for moving. — Visited probable new Dumps, Shops, Offices etc with DADOS 63rd. Visited 10.M. No.2. Workshops re ammunition for French	

Place	Date	Hour	Summary of Events and Information	Remarks and references to Appendices
Bruay	17th		Montana. To "Q" to learn "refilling pts" whilst moving.	NAM 1
	18th		To Arty Hd Qtrs re cancellation of indents. Then to Field Cashier. Called on DADOS. 63rd Division made final arrangements for transfer. Lorries commenced to move reserve stores to Barlin in the afternoon.	nary
Barlin	19th		Moved office to Barlin 9 am. + remainder of stores. 1.30 am moved shops. Visited D.A.Q. Several matters.	nary
	20th		Shops in working order. To Arty HdQtrs re deficiencies in gun parts. To D.A.C. re excess in kits. D.A.Q. re various questions. To Hd Qtrs of 63rd, 111th + 112th Bdes to settle the distribution of channels, achinery in toresession.	
	21st		Visited No.2 Workshops. + Heavy Mobile at Menville.	nary
	22nd		Arranged to billet the men in more suitable billets.	nary

Army Form C. 2118.

WAR DIARY
or
INTELLIGENCE SUMMARY.
(Erase heading not required.)

Instructions regarding War Diaries and Intelligence Summaries are contained in F. S. Regs., Part II. and the Staff Manual respectively. Title pages will be prepared in manuscript.

Place	Date	Hour	Summary of Events and Information	Remarks and references to Appendices
Bashi	22nd		Visited Hd.Qrs Div Adj re issue of gun transferred by Div.o.s 33rd Division. Issued 2,000 rounds S.A.A. to Bdes & Pioneer Batt. on instructions from "Q". Arranged with D.O.T.M. a more satisfactory system of relieving details for Madras Trench mountain batteries. D. it Q.	nil
"	23rd		Interview with our Div. Bath. Tramway to arrange for returns to be rendered to me in accordance with Trench Army Instructions. To 111th Bde Hd Qrs from 1st army re the provision of lamps for lighting the Colonne Tunnel, supply of rifle fire from enemy's grenades and other matters.	
"	24th		D.O.T.M visited 1st army's scrounging of Medium Trench Mortars for future use. Nothing of note during the day. At 10.15 PM "Gas Alarm" sounded. The men were paraded with	
	25th			nil

WAR DIARY
or
INTELLIGENCE SUMMARY
(Erase heading not required.)

Army Form C. 2118.

Place	Date	Hour	Summary of Events and Information	Remarks and references to Appendices
Bydin	25th	cont.	Three schools in the ready position. Roll called - every one present. Alarm sound is to be a falsa one — Parade then dismissed.	MM.
	26th		Visited Hd Qrs of each Brigade to ascertain if any Stokes Mortar cylinders had been discharged. To Merville with 3 discharged cylinders. Issued the undamaged cylinders immediately in return. To DHQ general admonition matter. Inspected Dump & Workshops. Arranged for unit's indent for winter underclothing for 15th Instructions. Arranged for issue to take place through O.C. Booths. Issued one 2" T.M complete 15" X "37 Med. T.M.B. to replace one damaged by shell fire. D.H.Q as usual.	MM
	27th		To No 2. Wkshps. re screwing of 2" Trench Mortars for Temple Silencers - work making progress. Visited D.O.T.M. D.H.Q as usual.	MM
	28th			MM

Army Form C. 2118.

WAR DIARY
or
INTELLIGENCE SUMMARY.
(Erase heading not required.)

Instructions regarding War Diaries and Intelligence Summaries are contained in F. S. Regs., Part II. and the Staff Manual respectively. Title pages will be prepared in manuscript.

Place	Date	Hour	Summary of Events and Information	Remarks and references to Appendices
Berlin	29th		Stone and Shute visited. To HdQrs 123 Bde RFA re excursion methods from Batteries of the Brigade. Called on O.C. Bathn regarding issue of anti-gas kit. Visited maneuvres through Div Baths. RFA as normal.	
"	30th		Stone & Shute visited. To O.C. Div Salvage to discuss organization of Salvage in the Division. A.D.O.S. called. Visited O.O. 4 Corps Troops re return of tents returnable & otherwise. O.C. 9th N. Staffs called. One re overhaul of equipment & Lewis guns. Rifle Inspection — all satisfactory. D.H.Q.	nary.

John Moresby
Lieut.
D.A.D.O.S. 37 Division

37/vol 14

C. 2118

D.A.D.O.S
37th Division.

War Diary for
October 1916.

37th Dˢ
5 · XI · 16.

John A. Mowatt
Lieut
D.A.D.O.S.

October 1916

Army Form C. 2118.

WAR DIARY
or
INTELLIGENCE SUMMARY.
(Erase heading not required.)

Instructions regarding War Diaries and Intelligence Summaries are contained in F. S. Regs., Part II. and the Staff Manual respectively. Title pages will be prepared in manuscript.

Place	Date	Hour	Summary of Events and Information	Remarks and references to Appendices
Barlin	Oct 1st		Visited store and shops. Explained the workings of the Department in this Division to Major Kid Harmon (attached 15 "Q" Branch for instruction). The supply of 4 2" Trench Mortars having been completed by No 2 Workshops, the vices were returned to D.O.T.M.	MAY
			To D.H.Q. - usual interview.	
Barlin	2nd		Various another month in office - "Gun supply up" stores and shops. To Merville - local punchers, + to obtain estimates for the supply of rifle covers.	mr
Barlin	3rd		Interview with Quartermasters of 8th Lincolns + 8th Somerset L.I. A.D.O.S. Called. To No 2. Mobile Workshop - then to Field Cashier 7th Corps. D.H.Q.	very
Barlin	4th		13 men reported at 10 am (1 from each Battalion) to be instructed in the repair of Gum Boots. Visited HdQrs 111th Brigade and HdQrs 63rd. Drummer and under mess clothing in bulk from Base.	very

T2131. Wt. W708—776. 500000. 4/15. Sir J.C. & S.

Place	Date	Hour	Summary of Events and Information	Remarks and references to Appendices
Bardin	5th		Gun boot clean finished - men returned to units. 5 Medium Trench Mortars sent to Henry Moliere Workshops for screwing (5 the Temple Silencers). To HdQrs 111th Bde re special stores for road. Then to HdQrs C.123RS RFA re deliv'y 2 dial sights. Transferred by 34 DROs	nil
Bardin	6th		D.H.Q. on various matters. To HQ 111th InfBde, 112 I.B. + 63rd I.B. Visited C.R.E and D.O.T.M.	nil
Bardin	7th		To LaBourse to interview D.A.D.O.S. 8th Div. - called at HdQrs R.A. on returning. Rifle inspection - all correct. Two Stokes Guns discharged by shell fire - wired base to A.D.O.S. - asked. Interviewed Salvage Officer re organization of Salvage. Drafted DROs for the return of unserviceable S.D. Clothing and the issue of Winter mode clothing.	nil
Bardin	8th		Another Stokes gun damaged by shell fire - demanded by wire from Base. To R.A. HdQrs	nil

WAR DIARY
or
INTELLIGENCE SUMMARY.
(Erase heading not required.)

Army Form C. 2118.

Place	Date	Hour	Summary of Events and Information	Remarks and references to Appendices
BARLIN	8th cont.		re Periscopes return. Drew 5" medium trench mortars from Workshops (where they had been screwed to take Temple silencers) and returned them to D.O.T.M. D.H.Q.	MTy
BARLIN	9th		D.D.O.S. 1st Army called and enquired thoroughly in to method of keeping office Records, and the working of the Stores & Divisional Shops in general. The DDOS was accompanied by the ADOS IVth Corps. To Divisional Laundry and No 2. Workshop. A 4 gun 4.5 Howitzer Battery from England joined the 126 Bde RFA - Recovery C.126. Two 3" Mortars destroyed.	MTy
BARLIN	10th		No 2 Ordnance Workshops leaving the area so made arrangements with No 8 at Ohain. Visited 63rd Reds HQrs.	MTy
BARLIN	11th		Stewart Ohpling Machines arrived from Paris in Bulk & were issued. To No 8 Ordnance Workshop - Then to 112th Bde Hd Qrs.	MTy

WAR DIARY or INTELLIGENCE SUMMARY

Army Form C. 2118.

Place	Date	Hour	Summary of Events and Information	Remarks and references to Appendices
Bailin	12th		Interviewed D.A.D.O.S. 27th Division. To C. 126th Bde R.F.A. (newly formed Howitzer Battery) to ascertain whether state of their equipment & harness is complete. Afterwards to DAC on similar matters re mobn. the DAC Section of this particular Battery. Visited HQ Divn. on return to Batteries etc of 5th Skoein Smiths at present with Divisional Trans. All 5" Stokes guns received in a deplorable condition necessitating the return to the Base of those demanded to replace. D.H.Q.	MM
"	13th		French Inspection form re ammn. mobil. Interview Quarter Master 13th Royal Fusiliers. D.H.Q.	MM
"	14th		D.A.D.O.S. 2nd Canadian Division called. Arrangy of with him gained 15th, over of harness ex-exped and spare not required. To Grenville 17th Heavy Mobile Workshop 15 sections Skoolows huns explain D.H.Q. Arrangd it to send all their 2 ammunition lack 15 mules in the morning.	MM

Army Form C. 2118.

WAR DIARY
or
INTELLIGENCE SUMMARY.
(Erase heading not required.)

Instructions regarding War Diaries and Intelligence Summaries are contained in F. S. Regs., Part II. and the Staff Manual respectively. Title pages will be prepared in manuscript.

Place	Date	Hour	Summary of Events and Information	Remarks and references to Appendices
BARLIN	15th		To Field Cashier to draw for Imprest. Interviewed D.A.D.O.S. 2nd Canadian Division. O.C B/126 Bde R.F.A called. Routine work and arranging for move.	MAY
"	16th		To Heavy Mobile Workshop with Shembos from cylinders for exchange. Made arrangements for refilling whilst units and on the move. Suspended issues from Base. D.H.Q.	MAY
"	17th		To LE CAUROY to arrange for dumping in advance, the Smoke Helmet and Sock reserves. Drew 3 2" Mortars from No 8 Ord. Wkshps and issued them to D.T.M. Their mortars had been screwed to the Temple Silencer. By No. 8 Ord. Wkshps. To BRUAY to interview D.A.D.O.S. 2nd Canadian Div. D.A.Q.	MAY
"	18th		Lorries to refilling point on the march. Moved 15 ROLLECOURT. Sent 3 lorries ahead 15 dumps at LE CAUROY so as to leave them free for refilling on	MAY

WAR DIARY
or
INTELLIGENCE SUMMARY.
(Erase heading not required.)

Army Form C. 2118.

Place	Date	Hour	Summary of Events and Information	Remarks and references to Appendices
ROLLECOURT.	18th	12.noon	cont. the manoeuvre. Carried on with usual work at ROLLECOURT.	MY
ROLLECOURT.	19th		Three lorries to BRVAY to draw 2,900 steel helmets for equipment reinforcements 215.	MY
LE CAVROY	20th		Office & personnel to LE CAVROY. Visited R.O.O. FREVENT to arrange reconsignment of Blankets which did not arrive in time to be drawn and issued. Arranged with "Q" to go in advance of Division to MARIEUX to prepare billets, accommodation for rest of Division for whom billets are not available.	MY
MARIEUX	21st		To MARIEUX. Arranged billets for personnel and accommodation for offices, store & shops with Town Major. Office & personnel arrived later. Interview with A.D.O.S. V Corps. Drew Extras as required by Division from O.O. V Corps Troops. W.O.'s to refilling P's places they	MY
MARIEUX	22nd		Issued Extras to Infantry Bdes at	MY

WAR DIARY
or
INTELLIGENCE SUMMARY.

Army Form C. 2118.

Place	Date	Hour	Summary of Events and Information	Remarks and references to Appendices
MARIEUX	22nd cont.		men stationed. Interviewed ADOS V Corps. W.O's to refilling points to interview Quartermasters of units.	MKy
"	23rd		Railhead changed from FRÉVENT to CONTEVILLE. New railhead is 17 miles distant and much too far to be practicable. Drew 1000 Blankets from Railhead to meet the needs of reinforcements. TO AMIENS to purchase material urgently required by Signals. W.O's to refilling points. D.H.Q.	MKy
"	24th		Inspected dumps and Shops thoroughly with view to making best arrangements possible in the event of Division receiving MARIEUX for some time. 4 Armourers, 2 Tailors and 2 Carpenters obtained through "Q" for work in Divisional Shops. Called on OO V Corps Troops. DHQ.	MKy
"	25th		Interviewed R.O.O. ACHEUX — then ADOS V Corps. Lorries to CONTEVILLE overnight. 8150 stores and 26 Lewis guns	MKy

Place	Date	Hour	Summary of Events and Information	Remarks and references to Appendices
MARIEUX	26th	cont:	arriv: on the movement. D.H.Q. Received and issued 26 Lewis Gun - 2 per Battalion. To Railheads to obtain empty biscuit tins to cut up for making distinguishing back patches from aeroplane observation. Consignment of 7 ton horseshoes and other stores notified by Base. Investigations regarding information of packsaddlery. Pack transport may become necessary in forward areas owing to the mud.	MM4 MM4
MARIEUX	27th		To A.D.O.S. Vth Corps - thence to No. 4 Casualty Clearing Station at VARENNES to collect small Box respirators. To FORCEVILLE to reconnoitre horsed position for advance of Armourers Shops, Dumps, DDOS Reserve Army and ADOS Vth Corps called - also Brig. Gen. Robinson (112th Inf Bde). Collected 40 sets pack saddlery from O.O. Vth Corps Troops. D.H.Q. interviewed D.A.D.O.S. 3rd Div.	MM7

WAR DIARY or INTELLIGENCE SUMMARY
Army Form C. 2118.

Place	Date	Hour	Summary of Events and Information	Remarks and references to Appendices
MARIEUX	28th		To ACHEUX with AA & QMG to inspect various forms of improvised packsaddling with view to producing same in Divisional Shops. Commenced manufacture of improvised packsaddles, water carriers and shell carriers in Divisional Shops. DHQ	may
MARIEUX	29th		General Potts (BGRA) called to inspect packsaddlery being made in shops. Notification of despatch from Bars of 19 tons of stores – arranged that transport to draw same from Railhead. Railhead changed to ST. LEGER Cx DOMARTS – still too far being finally obtained as CONTEVILLE.	may
MARIEUX	30.		Arranged with Town Major for the use of another barn for store purposes. Moved armourer's shop to more suitable premises. Consultation with ADVS re packsaddling. Bars notified despatch of 20 tons of stores. Arranged with transport	may

Army Form C. 2118.

WAR DIARY
or
INTELLIGENCE SUMMARY.
(Erase heading not required.)

Instructions regarding War Diaries and Intelligence Summaries are contained in F. S. Regs., Part II. and the Staff Manual respectively. Title pages will be prepared in manuscript.

Place	Date	Hour	Summary of Events and Information	Remarks and references to Appendices
MARIEUX	31st		ADVS VI Corps called & inspected dump, offices & workshops. Consignment of 16 tons of stores notified by base. In accordance with wishes of Q.O.C. of Division manufacture of tin funnels for use with water carts was undertaken by Divisional Shops.	MAY
			D.H.Q.	

Vol 15
37

War Diary for
November, 1916.

37th Division
24.12.16.

John H[?]
Lieut
for D.A.D.O.S.

Army Form C. 2118.

WAR DIARY
or
INTELLIGENCE SUMMARY.
(Erase heading not required.)

Instructions regarding War Diaries and Intelligence Summaries are contained in F. S. Regs., Part II. and the Staff Manual respectively. Title pages will be prepared in manuscript.

Place	Date	Hour	Summary of Events and Information	Remarks and references to Appendices
MARIEUX	1st		Notification received of despatch of 13 bin boots by Rouen and 5480 motorcycles, tun by Paris Railhead still at St Leger les Domart. 10 lorries were obtained through "Q" is being held being the 39 tins of stores from Railhead.	MM
MARIEUX	2nd		Conferences at Head Quarters re mobility operations - discussion of Administration Orders, Making arrangements for an advanced dump, officers & Armourers Shop at VARENNES. To AMIENS to Local Purchase, A.D.O.S. Vth Corps called & took away specimens of shell carrier for use with Pack saddles. D.W.H.Qrs.	MM
MARIEUX	3rd		Visited ADOS Vth Corps. — then to VARENNES 15 armoury with Town Major sit for advanced dump (Store tnt). Trial of hack saddle & mules carriers made in Armourer Divisional Shops - quite successful. D.H.Q.	MM
MARIEUX	4th		To DHQ to settle probational distribution to units of	MM

WAR DIARY
or
INTELLIGENCE SUMMARY.
(Erase heading not required.)

Army Form C. 2118.

Instructions regarding War Diaries and Intelligence Summaries are contained in F. S. Regs., Part II. and the Staff Manual respectively. Title pages will be prepared in manuscript.

Place	Date	Hour	Summary of Events and Information	Remarks and references to Appendices
MARIEUX	4th cont.		Andrews's Fur and Leather Jerkins. Cannier's 4.5 Howitzer arrived at Railhead also was in lunch R.E. Stone park. To AMIENS to Lorell Purchases - chiefly parts of Singer Sewing Machine. D.H.Q.	M.H.
MARIEUX	5th		Inspected dump & workshops thoroughly. D.H.Q. General Routine work.	M.H.
MARIEUX	6th		Despatch of 700 cases small box respirators notified by CALAIS. Referred question of priority of issue to 15" "Q". Settled on "SILS" for Stone Tent (for Armourers Shop & advanced Dump) at VARENNES. Interview with A.D.O.S. V Corps. Called on D.A.D.O.S. 63rd Division - discussed general arrangements - interchange of opinions & ideas. D.H.Q. - informed by A.A. + Q.M.G. that VARENNES will most probably not be used as advanced Div. Head Quarters, and that not all operations are likely to be arranged yesterday	
MARIEUX	7th		Majority of 15,000 Woollen drawers received	M.H.

Army Form C. 2118.

WAR DIARY
or
INTELLIGENCE SUMMARY.
(Erase heading not required.)

Instructions regarding War Diaries and Intelligence Summaries are contained in F. S. Regs., Part II. and the Staff Manual respectively. Title pages will be prepared in manuscript.

Place	Date	Hour	Summary of Events and Information	Remarks and references to Appendices
MARIEUX	7th		enemy issued. Learnt from "Q" that "operations" have been suspended indefinitely. Severe rain-traffic restrictions in force - consequently tons of stores had to be half-off-loaded-hand dumped at Railhead. 63rd Inf. Bde. move from BEAUVAL tomorrow. D.R.O.S and ADOS V Corps called in the morning and afterwards with 5 pr. of packsaddles found to be successful by 4th Army. Box Respirators received.	MARY
MARIEUX	8th		To Railhead ST. LEGER & BOMARTS. Arranged with Town Major for a Dump, and with R.T.O. for whatever lorries that arrive (whilst traffic restrictions are in force) to be unloaded and the stores dumped. Leaving our Cpl. A. G/C. L/Cpl- in charge of our lorry & its 2 drivers, which will remain at Railhead for purpose of transferring stores from Trucks to Dump. Men from Dy. Battalion in the	

Army Form C. 2118.

WAR DIARY
or
INTELLIGENCE SUMMARY.
(Erase heading not required.)

Instructions regarding War Diaries and Intelligence Summaries are contained in F.S. Regs., Part II. and the Staff Manual respectively. Title pages will be prepared in manuscript.

Place	Date	Hour	Summary of Events and Information	Remarks and references to Appendices
HARRIEUX	8th		return of Gunn Boots arrived also the 2 instructors. The instruction will take place in the stone tank pitched on the RANCHIVAL road. Heavy rain continues. D.H.Q. Commenced to issue Small Box Respirators according to priority given by "G" thereunto.	mry.
HARIEUX	9th		37 men from various units installed in the ref of 2 Instructors - instruction will continue tomorrow. Attached fatigue party for work on the road outside store. Fur Coats issued to 9th North Staffs (Pioneers) 2nd Blankets issued to D.A.C and Artillery units. D.H.Q. Informed by "Q" that 15 reinforcements will be "W" day. Weather showy and colder.	mry
HARIEUX	10th		Fine & Bright - "Q" confirm that today is an "W". Revised scheme for advanced Dump to an that all is in order. To Staff Captain R.A. Class for instruction	

WAR DIARY
or
INTELLIGENCE SUMMARY.
(Erase heading not required.)

Army Form C. 2118.

Place	Date	Hour	Summary of Events and Information	Remarks and references to Appendices
F/ARIEUX	10th		Certain repairs of Lynn Boat terminated. Station ready. Obtained 15 drawn + improve the sand adjoining the stove which had become saturated with drip.	nil
"	11th		in mud owing to recent rain. Today is "X" day. S.S. Packsaddles have been withdrawn by Corps from the Brigades – orders from "Q" to improvise as many as possible (?– "Q" obtained labour for this purpose from various units in the Division. Traffic restrictions removed.	nil
"	12th		Leave obtained through "Q" to clean dump at Railham. General Bruce Williams came into Boat Supply several men of 63rd Inf Bde having fallen out on the march owing to bad boots. Today "Y" day. D.H.Q. 15 to an final arrangements. To Advanced D.H.Q at VARENNES.	nil
"	13th		VARENNES -15 to be an advanced dump.	

WAR DIARY
or
INTELLIGENCE SUMMARY.
(Erase heading not required.)

Army Form C. 2118.

Place	Date	Hour	Summary of Events and Information	Remarks and references to Appendices
MARIEUX	13th	cont.	The Advanced dump will serve as a refilling point for 63rd Inf. Bde, will act as an Armourers shop for repair of Machine & Lewis Guns. Small reserve of important stores such as gun barrels, rifle oil, flannelette, socks is also being kept at this advanced Dump. Personnel at advanced Dump - Sub Conductor, 1 clerk & storeman, 4 Armourers. Issued 30 pack saddles informed in Div Shops - 10 head Brigade. Visited advanced Dump & DHQ at VARENNES.	mm
	14		Informed by Q that 37th Div taken over the line from 63rd Naval Division at 12 noon. Arrangements for movement of officers & dumps on the morrow. Visited Advanced dump at VARENNES and arranged to send it to Town Major HEDAUVILLE to employ officers Drew 100 GS pack saddles from 60 ? corps troops for distribution to 63 Inf. Bde.	mm

WAR DIARY
or
INTELLIGENCE SUMMARY.

Army Form C. 2118.

Place	Date	Hour	Summary of Events and Information	Remarks and references to Appendices
HEDAUVILLE	16th		Officer i/c dump of Reserves moved to HEDAUVILLE. 39th Divl. Artillery & 3rd Canadian Trench Mortars attached for administration — Sergeant clerk & storeman & 1 orderly marched from 39th DADOS for this purpose. To Advanced H.Q. MARTINSART to interview AA & QMG. Head Quarters, Rear Echelon moves from HEDAUVILLE to FORCEVILLE the morrow — preparations in now to FORCEVILLE.	Nil
FORCEVILLE	17th		Officer i/c Reserve Dump to FORCEVILLE. The 51st Tent near VARENNES still used as a refilling point for all units. 1700 Stun Coats issued to ea. Inf. Bde. To MESNIL to interview Officer in charge of Transport there to HAMEL to see Transport working with improvised packsaddles. Apparently pack improvised pack saddles are satisfactory — no sore backs. 111th M.G. Coy sent 1 Vickers Gun — one to replace used tom.	Nil
"	18h		The sum from units for mules, pack saddles received. 2 Lewis Gun on tyred & Shell fire. 18h gun with B.M. armed from A/179 Bde R.F.A. and was drawn by mules. To Advanced Hd Qtr and VARENNES (to see refilling at Stove Tent). Pas. B.10 Sh. 57d.	Nil
"	19h		To No. 24 Ordnance light Workshop to interview I.O.L. Drew this afternoon from O.O. V. Qts. for use at MESNIL Dump.	

A 5834 Wt. W4973/M687 759,000 8/16 D. D. & L. Ltd. Forms/C.2118/13.

Army Form C. 2118.

WAR DIARY
or
INTELLIGENCE SUMMARY.
(Erase heading not required.)

Place	Date	Hour	Summary of Events and Information	Remarks and references to Appendices
FORCEVILLE	19th cont		Interview with A.A. & Q.M.G. at Advanced Head Quarters.	nil
"	20th		1000 sets of underclothing delivered by lorry to O/C of MESNIL Dump for pack transport to 111th Bde. who were badly in need. To Advanced Head Quarters. 39th Div Arty moved back to 39th Div. lorry, sergeant clerk returned to Divs. 39th Div. To Advanced Head Quarters.	nil
"	21st			nil
"	22nd		Nothing of importance.	nil
"	23rd		To HAMEL and captured German Trenches with ADOS V Corps to see how the Salvage work was being carried on. Advanced D.H.Q. informed that we move back to MARIEUX 26th	nil
"	24th		To MARIEUX to arrange billetting of detachment, office stores + shops. 2 lorry loads of salved rifles, machine guns and captured German machine guns and Trench Mortars to Railhead from Salvage Dump MESNIL.	nil
"	25th		Arrangements for the move to MARIEUX. To VIGNACOURT to arrange embarkation from supply of Haynets. D.H.Q.	nil

WAR DIARY
or
INTELLIGENCE SUMMARY

Army Form C. 2118.

Place	Date	Hour	Summary of Events and Information	Remarks and references to Appendices.
FORCEVILLE MARIEUX	26/5		Moved to MARIEUX. Some difficulty experienced with the move owing to V Corps Traffic restrictions being in force.	may
MARIEUX	27"		To ADOS V Corps. Traffic restrictions removed. Second Blanket issued.	may
"	28/5		To DOULLENS to interview O/c of Officers Clothing Depot recently opened. D.H.Q. To Railhead BELLE EGLISE to interview R.O.O. Worked out scheme for refitting the Infantry Brigades of the Division. Balance of Leather Jerkins received from the Base + issued.	may
"	29/5		Pitched Store tent on RANCHIVAL – MARIEUX road and started Divisional Shoe's working therein.	may
"	30/5		Moved 9" N. Staffs (Pioneers) and 152 Fd Coy RE to 7" Division. It being impossible to advance them from MARIEUX. Nothing of importance.	may

2353 Wt. W2544/1454 700,000 5/15 D. D. & L. A.D.S.S. Forms/C. 2118.

Vol/16 Secret

War Diary
of
D.A.D.O.S. 37 Division
for
December 1916

John N Reynolds
Lieut
D.A.D.O.S

Army Form C. 2118.

WAR DIARY
or
INTELLIGENCE SUMMARY.
(Erase heading not required.)

Instructions regarding War Diaries and Intelligence Summaries are contained in F. S. Regs., Part II. and the Staff Manual respectively. Title pages will be prepared in manuscript.

Place	Date	Hour	Summary of Events and Information	Remarks and references to Appendices
MARIEUX	1st DEC.		Inspected Store Sheds. Medium and Heavy Trench Mortars of 3rd Canadian Division transferred back to DAPOS to Canadian. Issue of 2nd Blanket completed. Safety detail of refitting scheme – Divisional Head Quarters	nam.
"	2nd		To DOULLENS to m.s.v. – ADOS V Corps. – ADOS referred with me and inspected office records, store sheets, general and routine work. – Divisional Head quarters re outfitting. Refitting scheme issued to Division through "Q". Arranged for 63rd Infantry Brigade to send in all Lewis and Machine Guns for overhaul on programme devised so as to cause no interference with the training of Machine gunners. Monthly return of Bulk issues brought to notice of S.O.C. – the figures being unusually in view of tension during last month.	nam.
"	3rd		Inspection of Transport took place in accordance with Refitting Scheme – Subordinate Crawford at the disposal of 63rd Inf Bde to overhaul Transport not in subject in same. Railhead contd.	nam
"	4th			nam

WAR DIARY
or
INTELLIGENCE SUMMARY.

Army Form C. 2118.

Place	Date	Hour	Summary of Events and Information	Remarks and references to Appendices
MARIEUX	4th cont		changed to PUCHEVILLERS.	nil
"	5th		To HQ 111th Inf. Bde. re "Refilling Scheme" - all going well. Interview with O.C. 13th Rifle Bde. about various differences on company out- of recent action. Then to 112th R.A.M.C. - interviewed Q.O.C. and Staff Capt. Visited ADOS Vth Corps at DOULLENS to obtain further particulars of billets in charge of Town Major VAL-DE-MAISON. D.ADS to discuss provision of Divisional Baths and Laundries.	nil
"	6th		Thought-local Purchase at DOULLENS - 150th Inventory of Toulhy's at VAL DE MAISON. - Usual routine work. - Divisional HQrs. Usual routine work — nothing unusually important.	nil
"	7th 8th		Interviewed I.O. 75th Heavy Mobile Workshop at QUESNOY on question of wheels for Malka, cooks and Officers Mess Carts. Arranged	nil nil
"	9th		fallen account of in for Shafts + men. Immediate action was being nothing to keep notals from units for the refit. — otherwise nothing to note.	nil

Army Form C. 2118.

WAR DIARY
or
INTELLIGENCE SUMMARY.
(Erase heading not required.)

Instructions regarding War Diaries and Intelligence Summaries are contained in F.S. Regs., Part II. and the Staff Manual respectively. Title pages will be prepared in manuscript.

Place	Date	Hour	Summary of Events and Information	Remarks and references to Appendices
MARIEUX	10th		Usual routine work	nary
	11th		Informed by "Q" that Division will move from V Corps Area at short notice — Preparations from the move — To AMIENS 15000 forced Purchase. Visited D.A.D.Q. no further news — suspended issue from ROUEN and HAVRE.	nary
"	12th		Continued with preparations for move. Ambulances demanded from base. Premature 15th — 10th convoys demanded from base. D.H.Q.	nary
"	13th		Arranged with "Q" to have 2 x½a 3 ton lorries from the move — making 6 in all. List of units sent to CALAIS with instructions not to issue until notified. All ready to move on the morrow at 8 a.m. D.H.Q.	nary
FROHEN+LE-GRAND	14th		Moved Offices, Shops, Reserves and Personnel to FROHEN-LE-GRAND. Arranged with AA+QMG to proceed in advance of Division in order to be in a position to receive cont.	nary

WAR DIARY
or
INTELLIGENCE SUMMARY.

(Erase heading not required.)

Army Form C. 2118.

Place	Date	Hour	Summary of Events and Information	Remarks and references to Appendices
FROHEN-LE-GRAND	14th cont-		Stores as early as possible. "Q" arranged this matter with Corps	May
BETHUNE	15th		All six lorries left FROHEN-LE-GRAND at 8am. - self in advance by car. Lorries given instructions to park at BETHUNE and await instructions. Interviewed ADOS XI Corps at HINGES - visited LESTREM with ADOS - LESTREM will probably be D.A.Q. Billetted Office, stores, staff, and personnel in BETHUNE. Interviewed DADOS 5th Division - informed Signals and D.A.Q of location. Removed suspension on Base Railhead - BETHUNE	May
"	16th		Proceeded with usual routine work. ADOS XI Corps called also AA+QMG 5th Div.	May
"	17th		Stores drawn from Railhead. Took stock of everything in possession - nothing else of importance	May
"	18th		Arranged billets accommodation for office staff. Usual routine work.	May

Army Form C. 2118.

WAR DIARY
or
INTELLIGENCE SUMMARY.
(Erase heading not required.)

Instructions regarding War Diaries and Intelligence Summaries are contained in F. S. Regs., Part II. and the Staff Manual respectively. Title pages will be prepared in manuscript.

Place	Date	Hour	Summary of Events and Information	Remarks and references to Appendices
BETHUNE	19		Warrant Officers to refilling points with lorries and stores. Division arrived in XI Corps area. Artillery not yet. 154 Fd Coy RE was transferred to First Army Troops - have been detached from our Division.	MAY
"	20		Drafted DRO's for the trailmen by which - of warrantable Service Dress Clothing and Underclothing - arrangements different in this Corps Army. Warrant Officers to refilling points on Saturday. Informed by A.D.T.M.S that we want more boots. LESTREM 1200 prs Boots. Thigh drawn from DPDOS 5th Division.	
"	21		To HINGES to interview DDOS XI Corps - thence to LESTREM to army's accommodation from office, stays, stores and detachment. Moved all issuable stores to LESTREM, also 3 Warrant Officers + personnel - self and chief clerk remain at BETHUNE. ADOS XI Corps called in the afternoon. In accordance with Corps arrangements drew 6 rifle grenade coy	MAY

2353 Wt. W5441/1454 700,000 5/15 D. D. & L.   A.D.S.S. Forms/C 2118.

Army Form C. 2118.

WAR DIARY
or
INTELLIGENCE SUMMARY.
(Erase heading not required.)

Instructions regarding War Diaries and Intelligence Summaries are contained in F.S. Regs., Part II. and the Staff Manual respectively. Title pages will be prepared in manuscript.

Place	Date	Hour	Summary of Events and Information	Remarks and references to Appendices
BETHUNE	21st	cont-	Returns from R.E. workshops BETHUNE.	navy
LESTREM	22nd		Moved Office Shops &c to LESTREM — spent arrangements to settle down in new quarters. D.H.Q.	navy
"	23rd		Lt Taylor arrived to act for me whilst on leave. At 0.03 called. 1 machine gun destroyed by shell fire — demanded wire from Base. Went — thought all hopeless until Lt Taylor — handed over important document — intended leaving LESTREM by 10.45pm train from LA GORGUE — stopped by "Q" at 9.30 pm. All leave stopped until further notice. Carried on. Divisional Medal Queelits.	navy
"	24th		1 more machine gun damaged by shell fire — same Brigade — wired demand to Bases. Word received wants informed by "Q" at 1.30 pm that leave is again open via CALAIS. Final arrangements with Lt Taylor. Went on leave by 10.45 pm train from LA GORGUE.	why

Army Form C. 2118.

WAR DIARY
or
INTELLIGENCE SUMMARY.
(Erase heading not required.)

Instructions regarding War Diaries and Intelligence Summaries are contained in F.S. Regs., Part II. and the Staff Manual respectively. Title pages will be prepared in manuscript.

Place	Date	Hour	Summary of Events and Information	Remarks and references to Appendices
In the Field	Feb. 25		Going through papers left behind by M.S. hewrels — on receipt of wire from I.O.M. condemning 16/4 7th scoring Y. 4. 5. 7th check both repairable knotwork finning wires to replace — finding receipt 562 behives carried forward from Base arranging with S.S.O. to supply 13 K.R.R. with 58 hind jacks — enquiring as to consent of charge of billets townr to be made.	P25
	26		Hearing from R.T.O. Lt. GORNIE Ross on sealed truck & one open ph.tes including some ammunity removed shortly — 2 echo lories to close — visiting 6 KineCars — inspecting workshops & wire trend — arranging Sch duties of times for various pilot Grade to check outstanding wurkush — M.S.C. enquiring of sentry intervals for R.B. old be had limit explaining Field book broardown & knew even storage arrang & to see if we all land camp divisit — I.O.M. condemned 2 furniture 18 pdr for serving reprival to knotwork training wire to replace.	P25
	27		On receipt of circular from D.O.S. Htr. Stores all may come up from fum., one alternate days & enveloping propremme of firsh days to thommashing Bank store frepairing scheme for D.R.O. 15 empty with James — circular to A.O.S. kpg & Report B.S. to Dt. 1st of finish motors etc., & telescopic siphon & asking Supt store Templer Showse for 2" mortars — visiting then Railhead entertaining from W.O. M/C R.O. R.O.O. generally atturdet 2 days a week from BETHUNE: he reported all stand clear — meeting Capt. Hardham D.A.D.O.S 58c Divn — interview with O.M.S. of KingSon & he was to send all Lewis Guns to Divn Wshop to overhaul to finish — enquiring I.O.M. N° 21 workshop if X9 2 medium T.M. Gralls had sent in 2" mortars for overhaul.	P25

2353 Wt. W2541/1454 700,000 5/15 D.D.&L. A.D.S.S. Forms/C 2118

Army Form C. 2118.

WAR DIARY
or
INTELLIGENCE SUMMARY.
(Erase heading not required.)

Instructions regarding War Diaries and Intelligence Summaries are contained in F. S. Regs., Part II. and the Staff Manual respectively. Title pages will be prepared in manuscript.

Place	Date	Hour	Summary of Events and Information	Remarks and references to Appendices
In the Field	Sept 26		Wiring A.D.O.S and D' Aylward all carriages wagon limbers MK II — D.A.D.O.S 5½" stating he had met in train 766 fuzed bodies and 5 x A.D.O.S advised Army HQRs that interests within Corps arranging on phone NO 3 lines are old Letter & no interchangeable — instructing D.A.C. to hand over all springs running out 18/4 Q.F. 15. 10M N°21 workshops cutting on Town Major as to sites for testing being found there he did not exist — some wiring & Col. Pollard could not yet available — instructing 13 M.R.A.U. to attach 30 truck jacks from O.C. Dump — Instructing N° AD01 discussing one outstanding points — reporting ammunition with Supply Col. and 5 Armouring lorry with 5 M.A.C. & A.D.O.S arranged to send no correspondence this subject — engaged checking and issuing include 68 2d & 111 B group & obtaining certificates from units	A5
	29		O.C. X1 Corps Troops reporting 1500 5am brots for issue arranging to collect this afternoon asking Q for distribution — instructing pm L.C.B. for individual pamphlet 2 already in possession Q cable 1 wrote to units earliest Capt Blair reporting to Q Phase 2000 sets packed forward finished available O.C. X1 Corps Troops & Phase finally phoned M.G. & told the units the latter on 7 Day arms to send others for attaching note three — informing Q Phase additional 2.6.64 fm infr G Battn had been authorised — Phase 3 18/2024 arrived this morning — calling on 10M N° 21 workshop who informed he had overhauled 8 15 day NC returned 11 2" mortars — engaged checking and issuing include 112 B group & obtaining units' receipt	A6
	30		R.O.O. has Corps reports 3 18/2 not yet returned speaking to C.R.A. on phone & he promises to expedite matter — 5 Army being asked to hand over 1000 sets jackets etc. ready on L2.C.L. 3000 viriving distribution scheme accordingly — engaged checking outstanding include smith HQ group & obtaining units receipt cables & wires on bus — journey to Bethune trying wire cable & wires for Polish Sives	A7

2353 Wt W2544/1454 700,000 5/15 D. D. & L. A.D.S.S. Forms/C. 2118.

WAR DIARY
or
INTELLIGENCE SUMMARY.

Army Form C. 2118.

(Erase heading not required.)

Place	Date	Hour	Summary of Events and Information	Remarks and references to Appendices
In the Field	Oct 30 (cont)		Went to Schmitt to purchase animals unable to purchase having [illegible] — Saw Col H inspection 4.75 pm to Field Cashier to receive balance Frances 500 F.R. — on to Merville suitable hanging lamps not available the	AES
	31		Cuts Co Hospey stove with conduction instead of chimney — asking Q agent for distribution of 1500 firewood explaining owing to lack of stoves we will & there were chances are able to collect 3000 loads of firewood etc — L/N hours staying sometime before we leave arranging for these Wrote Col to Canal [illegible] staff on inspection — he from Corps to divisions 10 Div 1500 losses transferred Q 2 August 1500 from 3 Can Nil about 400 to repairs to depot Q ADDS who still insists on 12 infants on refer 1500 — ADDS permitted to hand in 1st Army as was on Q staff before — 4.5 Have not yet made arrangement [illegible] of animal.	AES
	1917 Nov 1		Notifying annual 24 hours frame to complete each Dept Rept to 12 noon. Inflating clamp map of undampt bags for carrying suffered to Q ref riding Receipt 150 Rupees came to the hospital Lt Col 2 hrs plates in line — inspecting was captured shut out rest collar of flag attacks & nothing in ... Capt on leaving came onto P and dined Col by ADMS & 1003 return arriving Col R.O 985 thursday manner of pkts etc.; list 253 Med Insp. Each Bde in line. Received on 1000 [illegible] 25 held by 2/ADDS as Divs Reserve as Fine Groves arriving into 1112 Fd Amb & R H are 12.00 5.15.	AES
	2		T.O.M continuing one shield upper fracture 4.5 send one 3" stokes mortar live shock III bde arriving Celais to replace — handled rapidly arrived 4.5 airing batting to Cathedral — 63rd battery came to deep from III & are left bde. Ren 8... [illegible] to find stretcher 1000 set packs 25 etc: notify us when ready to receive worry Celais one travelling kitchen 13 K.R.R. on [illegible] 9th... [illegible] wait to [illegible] from III bde and 12 lack of palisade for bro 15 wounded or infant from L/N [illegible] 75 luiers waiting to [illegible]

War Diary – 37th Division

Period Month ending 31st January, 1917.

3rd February, 1917.

John H. D. Powells
Lieut.
D.a.D.V.S., 37th Division.

WAR DIARY
or
INTELLIGENCE SUMMARY.

(Erase heading not required.)

Army Form C. 2118.

Place	Date	Hour	Summary of Events and Information	Remarks and references to Appendices
In the Field	1917 Jan 1		Notifying arrival 24 lorries from 16 complete coal Infantry Relief to 12 cwt; taking sample of bootproof bags for carrying water to GP infantry - weight 150 filled - one to be divided into 2 before it is put in - inspecting bootproof shield with system of flap attached working held wrapt ropes, being shown to GP and discussed by ADOS - receiving recept - orders to GP that shield to be to truck Bde in time - having met at [illegible] ordered with to R/y GP shield not to be to truck Bde in time - having [illegible] 1000 10th hastily DADOS as Div Reserve - three being - conveying with 112 Bde to deliver 1000 SAA at B&HQ tomorrow.	
		1.0 M.	Conversation re shield upper portion to 4.5" Y 1.3" lethal mortar shield of 111 Bde having Colas to inspect - shield upper portion arrived as being [illegible] if return - 63 destroy men today. From 111 Bn upper Bde 63rd arranged to find SAA for 1000 SAA gastropods & rifty upper Recorts to relieve - having Colins one travelling kitchen 13 KRR conveyed to	
	Jan 2	10 M -	Q travelling kitchens frm 112 Bde on account of shortage to being trundled in report from L.N.Lanes Y E.Lancs indicating upper shinny [illegible] work undertaken for 2 Units	

WAR DIARY or INTELLIGENCE SUMMARY

Army Form C. 2118.

Place	Date	Hour	Summary of Events and Information	Remarks and references to Appendices
In the Field	1917 Jan 2/Contd		Supply Officer had been short issued of 30 Zinc Cement, same for bags & hand been causing up site's posterity on interviews with Capt Harrison Staff Officers DDS this morning re Third Army. Taking of inventory postd. Sends to G + 10 and divisionals not to have on hand less than empty or return waxing for stable balance - also showed them minimum light for Heavy TM - and putting shops filled stores - only 100 trenches shields + Hartchell to be issued upon reg to depts. Leut Roberts running 100 at present rec'd 400 to return - running bag required and today arranging to complete this today to tomorrow - arranging with 112 Pde Trench - Showing Front 72 Wickets each day in Ammun Dept - undertaking for 6 unspecified to complete each NG by 24 hrs each - checking stock in store with Ledger.	R+5
	3		Storing 1000 Russian toll picks H.E. etc. collected from A.D. XI Corps Troops - have decided to issue all 200 trenches shields + weekly supply from huge Roberts - issuing over 50 in T.M.S. for instructional purpose - consequently must apply for from Coord. Ordnance. Stott had commd some workmen running K.R.R. estate Township Kitchener from Kitchener villers - including for M hand staff writing M 112 Bde A/A H.Q. Division's living Quarters with S.C. & explaining proposal for Entry reporting re Capt. 112 Warwicks & 58 Estonia came in as orderly officer for tomorrow - stop from A.D. XI Corps delivering 25 & 9 XI Pde.	R+5
	4			
	5		Returned from Leave previous evening — 11.45 P.M. — going through all corresp. have had a tremendous two - received during my absence on Leave. Lieut Taylor has left for duty at D.H.Q. Instructional stores and shops - also accumulation of NCO's men.	M-y

Army Form C. 2118.

WAR DIARY
or
INTELLIGENCE SUMMARY.
(Erase heading not required.)

Instructions regarding War Diaries and Intelligence Summaries are contained in F.S. Regs., Part II. and the Staff Manual respectively. Title pages will be prepared in manuscript.

Place	Date	Hour	Summary of Events and Information	Remarks and references to Appendices
LESTREM	5th cont. 6th		Capt Granville 10th Northum. Fus called as alteration of L/cmp/s F.S. Sanitary Officer. Called on Provision of Latrine Buckets – has been reports all in most places in this area enemy to watch. No 03/31 Pte W.S. Smith arrived from CALAIS to take place of Pte Bruce evacuated 10th June. 17 A or tupd Containers and 3 No 015/17 Stores received from Divnl Stores 56th Div. in accordance with instructions from XI Corps.	vary
"	7th		OC C/123 BdeRFA called re siege lamps of which there is a shortage – have received several this without result. Have routine work – nothing of special importance – D.H.Q.	may
"	8th		11 Stretchers received from "Base – "Q" asked us to their distribution. ADMS andADMS called to inspect accommodation of the detachment generally. ADMS advised me is be sent to obtain huts from the Divn – in fact the accommodation of Divn'nal Staff – present premises being very unsuitable in cold weather – submitted cont.-	may

2353 Wt. W2544/1454 700,000 5/15 D. D. & L. A.D.S.S. Forms/C 2118.

Army Form C. 2118.

WAR DIARY
or
INTELLIGENCE SUMMARY.
(Erase heading not required.)

Instructions regarding War Diaries and Intelligence Summaries are contained in F.S. Regs., Part II. and the Staff Manual respectively. Title pages will be prepared in manuscript.

Place	Date	Hour	Summary of Events and Information	Remarks and references to Appendices
LESTREM	8th	cont.	application to Division accordingly. 1 Limber GS Wagon (condemned by IOM) demanded from Base for 13th Rifle Bde.	nil
"	9th		Named Routine work. Chief Clerk (Sub Condr. Mason) went on leave to United Kingdom.	nil
"	11th		To Divisional Head Quarters. Lt Smitt Infantry Armourer attached to 1st Army, inspected the Divisional Armourers shop and enquired into the Armourers work generally. Usual routine work.	nil
"	11th		I Smitt visited the Brigade Head Quarters with me to obtain information as to how the Armourer Sergeant's attached to Infantry Battalions are employed by the Brigades. To Divisional Head Quarters re the abolition of the Lewis Gun Handcart and the consequent redistribution of Limber GS Wagons with Infantry Battalions.	nil
"	12th		New pattern Electric Army Push-Set issued to 14th Bty RA for trial and report. Nothing else of material importance.	nil
"	13th		To BETHUNE to local Purchase - calling at Cashier	nil

Army Form C. 2118.

WAR DIARY
or
INTELLIGENCE SUMMARY.
(Erase heading not required.)

Instructions regarding War Diaries and Intelligence Summaries are contained in F. S. Regs., Part II. and the Staff Manual respectively. Title pages will be prepared in manuscript.

Place	Date	Hour	Summary of Events and Information	Remarks and references to Appendices
LESTREM	13th	cont-	XIth Corps on the way. Inspected shops on a state thoroughly.	vary
"	14	"	Road from store to LESTREM flooded. ADOS XI Corps called. is discussion various question. Heads enlisted late road quite clear. To Divisional Head Quarters.	vary
"	15th		Nothing of unusual importance.	vary
"	16th		To BETHUNE Ist Armd Purchase. Visited First Army Heavy Mobile Gunnery Workshop at MERVILLE. Divisional Head Quarters.	vary
"	17th		To 111th Bde Hd Quarters to interview Staff Captain. Arranged with Staff Captain 63rd Inf Bde. (now out of the line) to renew all Machine Guns Spares of that Brigade, in Divisional Armourer's Shops.	vary
"	18th		To BETHUNE to lone a Purchase, – erected hut to provide more accommodation for Armourers. One 4.5" QF Howitzer demanded from Base by wire to replace one condemd by I.O.M. No 7 Workshot for each in home. (D/124 Bde RFA). To Divisional Head Quarters.	vary

Army Form C. 2118.

WAR DIARY
or
INTELLIGENCE SUMMARY.
(Erase heading not required.)

Instructions regarding War Diaries and Intelligence Summaries are contained in F.S. Regs., Part II. and the Staff Manual respectively. Title pages will be prepared in manuscript.

Place	Date	Hour	Summary of Events and Information	Remarks and references to Appendices
LESTREM	19th		Nothing of unusual importance.	
	20th		Visited Head Quarters 63rd Infantry Brigade to discuss various detachmental matters with Staff Capt. Divisional Head Quarters.	
"	21st		Butt Assistant Inspector of Armourers called & afterwards himself satisfied with arrangements made and been made for daily examination of the Armourers. A.A. & Q.M.G visited Officers Mess & shops in the afternoon. Nothing else of unusual importance.	
"	22nd		Chief Clerk Sgt. Major [?] on return from leave. Nothing else to report.	
"	23rd		Capt. Johnstone (with M.F.O.) called. Rifle, Kit & Gun Helmet inspection by Camp Commandant. 3 "Other Ranks" discharged by Hostile fire aircraft used by night. Divisional Head Quarters.	
"	24th		S.O. Hot food containers drawn from G.O.C. XI Corps Troops – also new type of spray for gas alarms. Nothing	

WAR DIARY
or
INTELLIGENCE SUMMARY.

Army Form C. 2118.

Place	Date	Hour	Summary of Events and Information	Remarks and references to Appendices
LESTREM	24th	cont.	Discussed with ADMS proposed form of Trench Stretcher made at canvas. Divisional Head Quarters.	M/4
"	25th		Report from "Q" through "Q" that whilst patrol suits unusual in recent raid but suspected material might be strong. To MERVILLE to enquire contact for Patrol Suits - thence to 2nd Army R.E. Shops to obtain sample of Thomas Box made by them (required for information of XI Corps "Q")	M/4
"	26th		50 Hut-foxed containers received from C.O. XI n Corps Troops went issued by tramp equally to the two Brigades in the line. Examined with D.A.D.M.S. with new type of stretcher for lifting wounded from narrow trenches + saps. Discussed Corps Scheme with ARMY. S. Divisional Head Quarters.	M/4
"	27th		Hand Routine Work - To BETHUNE to see ADut. Head Quarters.	M/4
"	28th		A.D.O.S. XI n Corps called - Base informed of re-organization of artillery - Divisional Head Quarters.	M/4
"	29th		To XI Corps Head Quarters - thence to BETHUNE to interview	cont.

Army Form C. 2118.

WAR DIARY
or
INTELLIGENCE SUMMARY.
(Erase heading not required.)

Place	Date	Hour	Summary of Events and Information	Remarks and references to Appendices
LESTREM	29th		D.A.D.O.S 5th Division informed us that 15 Heavy Mobile Workshop MERVILLE re Rifle Mechanism from 2" TM's. This man was instructed to A.D.O.S XI Corps – the workshop being at a greater distance than it is possible to replace – then Army gun unit of action.	many ✓
"	30th		Commenced erection of 2 Huts to accommodate Shop's + Personnel. Division and Head Quarters informed by A & Q.M.G. that a move is probable.	m ✓
"	31st		Endeavoring to be ready to move – 9 hours notice. Dispositions + arrangements according to Divisional Itand Quarters. To 1.8.17. No 21 Workshop at 2" Trench Mortain being fitted with new adaptors – there is Heavy Mobile Ordnance Workshop at MERVILLE is obtaining rifle mechanism from 2" Trench Mortars.	m ✓

37th Division.

War Diary for Month ending 28th February, 1917.

2nd March, 1917.

John H. [signature]
Lieut.,
D.A.D.O.S., 37th Division.

WAR DIARY or INTELLIGENCE SUMMARY

Army Form C. 2118.

Place	Date	Hour	Summary of Events and Information	Remarks and references to Appendices
LESTREM	1st February		To Divl Head Quarters – no further news. Confirmation with announcement for move. Transferred A/282 A.F.A. Bde to 5th Division and A/282 A.F.A. Bde to 56th Division. [The following were A/126 Bde R.F.A. + B/126 Bde R.F.A. him to recent re-organisation. D/123 + D/124 now have 6 4·5 Howitzers each.]	many
	2nd		To BETHUNE 15 interview 1.0 p.m. No 7 Kyreworking re vehicles in this shop belonging to this Division – amongst advantages Divl Head Quarters. – Suspended issues from the Base. Must Base 15 resume issues in 6 weeks, that more may be hardened. Division will be completely relieved tonight.	many
	3rd		Whole Division + Divisional Artillery now out of the line – 63 F.A. & R.A.O. is usefully point with Corny – other units still drawing from Dump. To Field Cashier – then to MERVILLE 15 annexes, collect for distr., making Armbands and Patches. Divl Head Quarters. Interview with D.T.M.O. – nothing of exceptional importance.	many
	4th		– Divisional Head Quarters.	many

Army Form C. 2118.

WAR DIARY
or
INTELLIGENCE SUMMARY.
(Erase heading not required.)

Instructions regarding War Diaries and Intelligence Summaries are contained in F. S. Regs., Part II. and the Staff Manual respectively. Title pages will be prepared in manuscript.

Place	Date	Hour	Summary of Events and Information	Remarks and references to Appendices
LESTREM	5th		S.S. Helmets Stall outfit chain irons received - also Horse rugs 15 complete. Division. 24 Lewis Gun received - 2 ½ a per Battalion. ADOS XI Corps called. Divisional Head Quarters - no news.	mm
"	6th		Accompanied S.O.C. on inspection of D.A.C. - visited Staff Captain R.A. and DOTTY. no mention of going by I.O.M. Divisional Head Quarters - AA & QMG stated that we move 15 I Corps Area in 2 or 3 days - (probably take over from 24th Div. - Head Quarters near le VIEUX LES MINES.	mm
"	7th		Kit and Rifle inspection. Capt Roberts on DADOS 5th Division called. Divisional Head Quarters instd of this Division later and from 24 Div. on 8th instant (tomorrow) relief will be completed night 13th - 14th. Head Quarters move on the 14th to HAZINGHIRBE, BRAQUEMONT.	mm
"	8th		Arrangements to refill (ordnance) these units which will be out of their area in a few days. To BRAQUEMONT to interview DADOS 24th and to make arrangements from taking over. Discovered that DADOS was on leave but encountered ADOS I Corps coming out of the office - 24 Ordnance will cont.	

Army Form C. 2118.

WAR DIARY
or
INTELLIGENCE SUMMARY.
(Erase heading not required.)

Place	Date	Hour	Summary of Events and Information	Remarks and references to Appendices
LESTREM	8th		He called in evening of the 11th. Shall take over morning of the 12th — moving the office finally on the 13th instant. Divisional Head Quarters — returned and announcing me as etc.	mmg
	9th		D.H.Q. — no new developments — returning to Base 2 GS wagons, 3 cooks carts, 2 Water carts, 1 Machine & Telephone wagon to me in organization in a. Nothing else of moment importance.	mmg
		10.15	Returned 1000 sets S.D. clothing to OYO X¹ Corps Reserve. Adjutant 9th N. Staffs called re. stores in area. Divisional Head Quarters.	mmg
		11th	All 3 Brigade Groups refilled at ASC refilling points by trains. To HINGES, to new fm — refused — then to BRAQUEMONT. Withdrew DADOS 24th Division and made several arrangements for taking over. Transferred about 80 Lewis Gun Handcarts (which became surplus on reorganization of Lewis Gun Transport) to DADOS 56 Division — 12 GS. Wagons returned by Dual Train on surplus on & reverted to	mmg

WAR DIARY
or
INTELLIGENCE SUMMARY.
(Erase heading not required.)

Army Form C. 2118.

Place	Date	Hour	Summary of Events and Information	Remarks and references to Appendices
LESTREM	11th	cont	Anti-aeroplane organization – ordered items, 1st Railhead, Armourers Shop, Smoke Helmet, Respirators & Sock reserve loaded ready 15 min off at 7 am tomorrow for BRAQUEMONT. Divisional Head Quarters.	my
"	12h		Lorries to BRAQUEMONT – 7 am. (One will clear new Railhead if a hint has arrived – ammunition returning empty) Truck arrived at NEUX LES MINES – cleaned and unloaded with new stove. Divisional Head Quarters. All lorries loaded for the morrow with exception of one to be loaded with Office & cook-house at 8 am tomorrow – other 3 lorries leaving for BRAQUEMONT at 7 am on the morrow.	my
BRAQUEMONT	13h		3 lorries left at 7 am – Office & cook-house at 8.30 am. Inspected premises occupied and saw that all were left perfectly clean. To BRAQUEMONT – took over office from 24th Ordnance. To BETHUNE Munitions electric lamps for Armourers Shop and Office. Divisional Head Quarters.	my
"	14h		Settling down generally. 6 units transferred from DADOS 29th Div.	my

Army Form C. 2118.

WAR DIARY
or
INTELLIGENCE SUMMARY.
(Erase heading not required.)

Place	Date	Hour	Summary of Events and Information	Remarks and references to Appendices
BRAQUEMONT	14th	cont.	Thorough inspection of all Billets, Cooking arrangements, Shops, Offices and Store. To SIVENANT is interview Commandant 47th Divl School of Instruction & is take steps allotted to O.H.Q. Called on Salvin in office re arrangements for return by units of innumerable S.D. Clothing & General Stores. Divisional Head Quarters.	mry
"	15th		A.D.O.S. 1st Corps called - reviewed with me system of working in 1st Corps. To BILLERS to hear lecture on Divisional arrangements (Administrative) made by a Division during the offensive on the SOMME. — Divisional Head Quarters.	mry
"	16th		Visited 112th Staff Captain. Item Staff Capt. 63rd Inf Bde. - afterwards to BETHUNE for local purchase. A.A. & Q.M.G. called, also O.C. B.th R.R.S. — Divisional Head Quarters.	mry
"	17th		Interviewed A/12 Bde R.F.A. - re excision incidents. Trouble with rifle mechanism, had difficulty in technical the supply. To MERVILLE with damaged 2" Trench Mortar and to obtain more rifle mechanism. Called at 10 Sqn. cont.	mry

WAR DIARY
or
INTELLIGENCE SUMMARY.
(Erase heading not required.)

Army Form C. 2118.

Place	Date	Hour	Summary of Events and Information	Remarks and references to Appendices
BRAQUEMONT	17	cont.	No. 1 Ordnance Workshop transferred hereto at Spring's relief by No. 21. Two men D.A.C. Demison died 2,300 trans of gun boots freight from leave on special enterpot (by wire). Died Head Quarters. 3" Stokes demanded by wire - shortage by breakage.	my
"	18th		Stokes Gun (on what remains) returned by 112" T.M. Battery from despatch to Base. To 1.O.M. No. 1 Workshop BETHUNE 2 washers for rifle mechanism. Interviewed DADOS 5th Division. Collected captured machine gun from OC XI Corps Troops. Two were for instructional purposes. Interviewed Adjutant 13 K.R.B. & Adjutant Divisional Trench Mortars."	my
"	19		Transport Officer 63rd Bde. called re hack saddling. Urgent demand for more cordite space at Armourers Shop - for special stores.	my
"	20th		To No. 1 Ordnance Workshop BETHUNE re 2" Trench Mortars. Attended Lecture at LILLERS by Maj. Gen Lord on "Regards for offensive action from the Corps Point of view." Interview my	e unit.

Army Form C. 2118.

WAR DIARY
or
INTELLIGENCE SUMMARY.
(Erase heading not required.)

Place	Date	Hour	Summary of Events and Information	Remarks and references to Appendices
BRAQUEMONT	20th		with A.A.Q.M.G.	mss
"	21st	1800 hrs	Visited Staff Capt. 63rd Inf Bde. - Then to BETHUNE to Local purchase. 1800 hrs Gum Boots Thigh received + distributed Div'l Head Quarters.	mss
"	22nd		Visited No 1 Ordnance Workshop BETHUNE and Turkery Heavy Ordnance Workshop at MERVILLE. Went to Rectice at LILLERS by Bus. 9 pm. MAY. D.O.O.T.M. called. Divisional Head Quarters.	mss
"	23rd		Interviews with O.C. 112th Trench Mortar Battery, O.C. D/62 and Staff Captain R.A. Thorough inspection of shafts + wheels. Railhead Ordnance officer called. To BETHUNE 15 purchase soap for Baths - supply being run out. Divisional Head of Quarters.	mss
"	24th		To Field Cashier 1st Corps - Then to SAILLY-LA-BOURSE to A.D.O.S. 1st Corps conference. - Saw D.A.D.O.S. 21st Division, General amongoments. Conference with Staff Captain R.A. and Adjutant D.A.C. on system of indents. Divisional Head Quarters.	mss

WAR DIARY
or
INTELLIGENCE SUMMARY.
(Erase heading not required.)

Army Form C. 2118.

Place	Date	Hour	Summary of Events and Information	Remarks and references to Appendices
BRAQUEMONT	25th		To MERVILLE – First Army Heavy Ordnance Workshop: – then to No.1 Light Mobile Ordnance Workshop BETHUNE. Conference at Divisional Head Quarters with A.D. + Q.M.G. re convoy move in 5th out- (advance answer mouse) for inclusion in Administrative Orders.	mry.
"	26th		O.C. 106th Bde. B.A.C called – also O.C. A/158 and A/123. Bde.R.F.A. put in claims for new magnus Divisional Head Quarters. 1 Vickers gun discharged by shell fire. Nothing else of unusual importance.	my
"	27th		To LABUISSIERE - 15 s+4 moor. I loaf, and Ordnance Officer 1 Cwt Transports. Then to DIEVAL 24th Divn. 15 am arrived this fatay owen. ADOS 1 Cwts tonight 2nd Lieut Lewis AOD (Boot s/ht.) – he stays with this Division 2 days 5 am 9h – 15 inst'd. Remainder Shoemakers Shop 5. Divisional Head Quarters.	my
"	28th		2nd Lieut Lewis went round the whole of the Battalion Shoemakers Shops. To ROLLECOURT re become a c/ manu/k with the 2nd + 15th Div'n. Division is moving in morning on 1 15	

Army Form C. 2118.

WAR DIARY
or
INTELLIGENCE SUMMARY.
(Erase heading not required.)

Instructions regarding War Diaries and Intelligence Summaries are contained in F. S. Regs., Part II. and the Staff Manual respectively. Title pages will be prepared in manuscript.

Place	Date	Hour	Summary of Events and Information	Remarks and references to Appendices
BRAQUEMONT	28th Cav	5.5E	what ammunition was necessary to accommodate Stores, Workshops, Offices etc. form of DADOS in ROLLECOURT - reported here to inform me by wire when he intended to move units. To VI Corps Hd Qr 1st Infantrie Divs. 2nd Head Quarters.	

J H Murray Lt
4.96 DOS
28 Aug

37th Division.

War Diary for month ending 31st March, 1917.

John H. Howards
Capt.
D.A.D.O.S., 37th Division.

WAR DIARY or INTELLIGENCE SUMMARY

Army Form C. 2118.

Place	Date	Hour	Summary of Events and Information	Remarks and references to Appendices
BRAQUEMONT	MARCH 1st		In accordance with instructions from ADOS I Corps transferred 2nd Lieut Lewis (Army expert) to DADOS 16th Division, 21st Division, ADOS I Corps called and inspected Office Shops Store & Hospital Samples. AA&QMG 15th Division to arrange for their DADOS to receive from Ordnance Store at ROLLECOURT & to field centres 1st Corps — thus to ADOS with Lieut Lewis & OO (Kent Expert) — to DADOS 24th Div. and ADOS I Corps — Boots & Helmets called on DADOS 6th Div to arrange to take the 15th	my
"	2nd		men of my Imprest Office Store Shops on the 4th instant. Issued Requisition. Transferred 108 AFA Bde to DADOS 6 Div. Railhead changes to LILLERS Tomorrow — visited Railhead of LILLERS. To ROLLECOURT — DADOS 15th Division still to Ordnance Store — which took the in own area on the 4th. — Informed AA&QMG of this fact — AA&QMG 16th Division (15th) to arrange for their DADOS to receive (2nd inst). Transferred all attached units to DADOS 6th Div.	my
"	3rd			
"	4th		Inspected Shoes & Shops so as to leave premises clean for DADOS 6th Div — who came today are now at 11 AM	my

Army Form C. 2118.

WAR DIARY
or
INTELLIGENCE SUMMARY.
(Erase heading not required.)

Instructions regarding War Diaries and Intelligence Summaries are contained in F. S. Regs., Part II. and the Staff Manual respectively. Title pages will be prepared in manuscript.

Place	Date	Hour	Summary of Events and Information	Remarks and references to Appendices
BRAQUEMONT MORRENT -FONTES	4th		General affair at MORRENT-FONTES at 2pm – Railhead LILLERS. Amount of baggage moved to Roellecourt tomorrow – Store of baggage forwarded. Sgt Luscombe direct from BRAQUEMONT. Divisional Head Quarters	my
ROELLECOURT	5th		To ROELLECOURT arrived accommodation for all full-strength. 17.45pm pantry departure of DADOS 15th Division. VI Corps informed DHQ that DADOS 15th Div will vacate ROELLECOURT in all stretch. Stores and shops transferred from BRAQUEMONT	—
	6th		Remained three know up from BRAQUEMONT. TO BRAQUEMONT 5.49 all clear. 18th 3rd Cut night to A/23 confirmed by	my
"	7th		1.017 – confirmed for me to advance – AA 979 called. VI Corps Head control work with am and instructed officers arrived who returned with am and instructed officer arrived.	my
"	8th		D.A.D.O.S. 15th Div. moved to DUISANS – moved stones from hand. Over 15th that V.I. GA by DADOS 15th Div – similarly moved office. DHQ arrive tomorrow.	my
"	9th		Store & shops in working order – various attention to make Store shops more convenient. D.H.Q. arrived.	my

Army Form C. 2118.

WAR DIARY
or
INTELLIGENCE SUMMARY.
(Erase heading not required.)

Instructions regarding War Diaries and Intelligence Summaries are contained in F.S. Regs., Part II. and the Staff Manual respectively. Title pages will be prepared in manuscript.

Place	Date	Hour	Summary of Events and Information	Remarks and references to Appendices
ROELLECOURT	10th		2.5a Lewis Gun per Infy Battalion reserve issued. — Railhead FRÉVENT — All steps concentrating on various devices for use with Pack Transport — Interview with M.T.O. & Q.M.G. re Pack Transport.	—
"	11th		Interviewed Quartermasters of 5th Lincoln + 10th Royal Fusiliers. — Conference on Divl Head Quarters on the provision of Pack Transport and other matters in connection with coming operations.	—
"	12th		Vickers Gun demanded from the Base to replace one condemned in Divl Armourer's Shop. VII Corps ruling that demands for stores in Sect. in IA (5+6 and to be sent to Havre from 14th instant (with the exception of stores in Sect. 16B) — Notified units to submit separate indents. Amended conference of D.A.D.O.S. & VI Corps Head Quarters.	—
"	13th		1500 Boxes for Box Respirators received from the Base — usual routine work.	—
"	14th		Specimen mustering flag for Rentoul approved by DHQ. — manufacture of same commenced in Divl Shops.	—
"	15th		Barrels + Cups demanded from the Base in accordance with GRO. 2181. Notified Divl Arty, T.R.A.C. that indents for Gun parts may only be submitted by D.A.C.	—
"	16th		Moved all units of 37 Divl Artillery to O.O. VII Corps Troops — returned to Base a surplus Lewis Gun Salved by 5th Lincolnshire Regt.	—

Army Form C. 2118.

WAR DIARY
or
INTELLIGENCE SUMMARY.
(Erase heading not required.)

Instructions regarding War Diaries and Intelligence Summaries are contained in F. S. Regs., Part II. and the Staff Manual respectively. Title pages will be prepared in manuscript.

Place	Date	Hour	Summary of Events and Information	Remarks and references to Appendices
BOELLECOURT/16		cont:	In accordance with instructions forwarded to Divisions intent for 1000 fathoms of cordage for transmission to VI Corps. Wired Heavy Mobile Workshops to know whether any 2nd Class C No 2010 wheels were available - reply "No". Collected from 60 VI Corps Tracts 400 sacks Bayonet fights from Divl School of Instruction. 14 Army R/51.26 + 1 compass (Observation Post) were also collected from 27 Divl Artillery.	my
"	17th		Corps Laundry at FREVENT made 15 reliefs serious situation regarding exchange of under clothing - Special demand sent to the Base for 2,000 sets. 3,500 7ds at W.b Hemps demanded from the Base for manufacture of "Trench hose" (or "Yukon Canvass") in Divisional Shops - matter being urgent Local Purchase was tried but prices were too high - Conference on "Packsaddlery" at 63rd I. Brigade Head Qrs - various authorisations shown - discussions on 15 minit of different types.	my
"	18th		2nd Gud. Q.F. 18 hrs No 5570 without B.M. received from A/123 Bde R.F.A. -	my

WAR DIARY
or
INTELLIGENCE SUMMARY.
(Erase heading not required.)

Army Form C. 2118.

Place	Date	Hour	Summary of Events and Information	Remarks and references to Appendices
ROELLECOURT	18th cont.		- also a Vickers M. Gun for 63rd Machine Gun Coy. 4,36,000 Dummy Cartridges S.A.A. were collected from O.O. VI/7 Corps Troops - "Q" asked for distribution.	my
"	19th		Usual routine work. Demanded from the Bone a Vickers Gun and Tripod to replace similar stolen condemned by Ord. Armourers Sketch.	my
"	20th		Informed by "Q" that 37th Div Adjg is attached to 21st Division as a temporary measure. A.D.O.S. VI Corps given particulars of the last arrival of trucks containing Ordnance Stores - "Bulk Issue" trucks only.	my
"	21st		Interview with A.A & Q.M.G. - attended trial of improvised Pack-saddlery by C.R.E.	my
"	22nd		O.C. 63rd Machine Gun Coy called re adaption for the use of the Lewis Gun with Anti-Aircraft Mountings. D.D.O.S. Third Army stopped on his way past the Store 16 enquired re make enquiries re Trench Stores demanded by 1st Division. Spoke A.A & Q.M.G re extradition - (Special Stores required).	my

Army Form C. 2118.

WAR DIARY
or
INTELLIGENCE SUMMARY.
(Erase heading not required.)

Instructions regarding War Diaries and Intelligence Summaries are contained in F.S. Regs., Part II. and the Staff Manual respectively. Title pages will be prepared in manuscript.

Place	Date	Hour	Summary of Events and Information	Remarks and references to Appendices
ROELLECOURT	23rd		Discussion of various Estimates questions with quartermasters of 8th Lincolns and 13th KRRC. - Issued iron rations for water carriers (made in Divisional Shops) in accordance with distribution decided on by "Q".	mu
"	24th		To 63rd Infy Bde Hd Qrs. 15 an army's provision of improvised packsaddles – then to ADOS VI Corps. Interview with AA+QMG re funding of mules.	mu
"	25th		During a sham farmhouse the Lewis Gun, to be convenient, of fired from the hip, and is to be carried slung from the shoulder. Cleaned truck at LABRET – truck heavy, arrived at their railhead by error. – Divisional Head Quarters.	mu
"	26th		Attended a conference of DADsOS at Head Quarters VI Corps. – Nothing else of unusual importance.	mu
"	27th		Interview with OC. 50 Field Ambulance re packsaddlery. contn:-	mu

A.5834. Wt. W.4973/M687. 750,000 8/16 D. D. & L. Ltd. Forms/C.2118/13.

WAR DIARY or INTELLIGENCE SUMMARY

Army Form C. 2118.

Place	Date	Hour	Summary of Events and Information	Remarks and references to Appendices
ROUGE COURT	27th		Discussed with AA & QMG provision of special stores for hunting operations. Divisional Head Quarters Café.	—
"	28th		To AMIENS to love Purchase - completed dishevelment flags for Infantry Platoons - Interview with AA & QMG 50th Division.	—
"	29th		Hand written work - collected 100 pairs of Gum Boots and 375 Shell Helmets with chin-tassens from Gochamere. Officer VI Corps Troops. Divisional Head Quarters.	—
"	30th		Inspection of fan lights appliances of AOC & men attached. Discussion re Pack saddlery with O.C. Divl Train. Demonstration of the use of Lewis Gun Slings (for fire from the hip) for the benefit of Quartermasters 8th Lincolns & 13th KRRC.	—
"	31st		Notified that Railhead changes to DUISANS on the 2nd Prox. – All mounts to HAVRE + ROUEN as Divisional now based on Southern Beach. To Corps Head Quarters to ask ADOS if small arm section detached from own DAC may be truckled as a unit by the Base the remainder of the DAC being with DAD OS 4th Division – Left on the Corps a specimen of improvised hand-	—

Army Form C. 2118.

WAR DIARY
or
INTELLIGENCE SUMMARY.
(Erase heading not required.)

Place	Date	Hour	Summary of Events and Information	Remarks and references to Appendices
ROLLECOURT	31	cont:-	cont:- saddle - also another type of Bombing Route made in Division al shops. Visited AGNES en DUISANS is our new Railhead and also site of D.H.Q. when we move up; Divisional Head Quarters.	m

37th Division.

War Diary for month ending 30th April, 1917.

37th Division.
1-5-1917.

John H. Roworth
Capt.,
D.A.D.V.S.

Army Form C. 2118.

WAR DIARY
or
INTELLIGENCE SUMMARY.
(Erase heading not required.)

Instructions regarding War Diaries and Intelligence Summaries are contained in F.S. Regs., Part II. and the Staff Manual respectively. Title pages will be prepared in manuscript.

Place	Date	Hour	Summary of Events and Information	Remarks and references to Appendices
ROLLECOURT	APRIL 1st		Commenced manufacture of "Tump lines" and Lewis Gun Slings in Divisional Shops - Railhead changes from FREVENT to AGNES-les-DUISANS tomorrow. Divisional Head Quarters - authority received from D.D.O.S Third Army to demand 1200 fathoms of Manilla Rope from the Base. Division now based on Southern Bases.	MM
"	2nd		To ST.POL + FREVENT to purchase stores urgently required for coming operations. Visited I.O.M. Heavy Mobile Work Shop:- a fitting of 3" Trench Mortars with deflection scales. Issued 90 Tump lines to each Infantry Brigade, also 226 fathoms of rope for packsaddlery. Interview with A.A + Q.M.G. re operations.	m
"	3rd		Arrangements to find best way of using Blankets for bivouacs. - D.A.D.M.S and Divisional Machine Gun Officer called. Divisional Head Quarters.	mm
"	4th		By car to AGNES les DUISANS to arrange site for stone laying dump - picked stone laying and arranged new reserves from ROLLECOURT - Leaving a party in charge. Interview with D.A.D.O.S 12th Div. Drew supplies from Field Cashier and went to VIGNACOURT to draw contract from Hospitals. Arranged RTO	mm

A3834. Wt. W4973/M687. 750,000 8/16 D. D. & L. Ltd. Forms/C.2118/13.

Army Form C. 2118.

WAR DIARY
or
INTELLIGENCE SUMMARY.
(Erase heading not required.)

Instructions regarding War Diaries and Intelligence Summaries are contained in F. S. Regs., Part II. and the Staff Manual respectively. Title pages will be prepared in manuscript.

Place	Date	Hour	Summary of Events and Information	Remarks and references to Appendices
ROLLIECOURT	4/4/17		15 mm [?] all but Tailors and Armourers Shops on the move to AGNES.	m
AGNES les DUISANS	5/4		Moved Office and Stores to AGNES lez DUISANS. – Built shelters and made several arrangements for arrival within Bn. M. T. lorry buckets in AVESNES le COMTE there being arrangely accommodation for stores. Drew 45 sets of G.S. had saddling from D.A.D.O.S. 14th Div and issued to accompany 15 distribution Svee by Head Quarters of the Division. Interview with A. & Q.M.G. obtained hour from APM 15th Division for Garriaerce Lorries to use the AGNES & WORRUS road in both directions – this being a "one way" road of Ordnance Dump being only 3 Kilometres from AGNES end.	m
"			To ROLLIECOURT 15 armoury for Armourers and Tailors Shops. To AGNES les DUISANS – afterwards to BRUAY and BETHUNE to purchase novels for Divisional Shops. Divisional Head Quarters on matters in regard to operations. Informed Hd Qrs but Bden, CRE and ADMS. what Ordnance Stores were yet did to be at Divl Dumps on "Y" day.	my

WAR DIARY
or
INTELLIGENCE SUMMARY.

Army Form C. 2118.

Place	Date	Hour	Summary of Events and Information	Remarks and references to Appendices
AGNES & DUISANS	7th		Collected from O/C VI Corps Tps. MGO Waistcoats from Grenade Carriers and issued them to 63rd Inf. Bde. – Issued 2,000 sets of underclothing to O/C Gym Park, FREVENT. A.D.O.S. VI Corps called & visited dumps. Divisional Head Quarters.	mm
	8th		To 10th No. 25 Workshop DUISANS – Drew 15 111" & 112" HE Shells. 15 delivery Levers, Gun Slings, & 15 discs. Grave matters generally with respect to the attack – to-day being "Y" day. Delivered 29 Panniers to HE Shells in accordance with instructions from "Q". Issued Buckets & rope for drawing water from wells in expiation – limiting to Advanced Dumps. Truck arrived from	mm
	9th		ROVEN at 11.0 am – cleared at 5.30 am. VI Corps attacked 2.3 Stokes Guns finally at – 2 AM 9-4-16 collected at ____ from 1.0.M. No 25 Grenade Workshop DUISANS. Truck arrived w. Railhead 9.0 pm cleared. 110 Stretchers issued to 49th Field Ambulance. Macintosh Capes finished for Army – reported completion VI Corps. Park of Levers & Pickers, Guns and Parts of 3" Stokes Mortars demanded from Grenade Gym Park FREVENT – demands for these have having been cancelled by the Base in accordance with Third Army letter.	mm
	10th		To ADOS VI Corps – drew items to FREVENT 1055. Gun ammunition	mm

Army Form C. 2118.

WAR DIARY
or
INTELLIGENCE SUMMARY.
(Erase heading not required.)

Place	Date	Hour	Summary of Events and Information	Remarks and references to Appendices
AGNEZ LES DUISANS	10th	cont:-	Gun Parks. Sent a Warrant Officer with 2 men to advanced Divisional Dump with Divl Reserves of Ordnance Stores. Considerable advance having been made it may become necessary to move nearer the Guns in any moment. Preparations made to meet this contingency.	
"	11th		To Ordnance Dump at BLANGY. It is that arrangements were satisfactory. Went onto the captured German lines to see Packsaddling in use and is not known. (Advanced) Head Quarters (advanced) at Salway's department. To Divisional Head Quarters in the Horseshoe Camp ARRAS - There intimated the D.A.D.O.S. Louis Gun Complete and 4 Vickers Gun Tripods handed in from advance Gun Ponds PREVENT. Three shunt towing been destroyed in action. 3" Stokes Gun reported unserviceable also Mess Cart (Complete Turnout), also 2 Officers Saddles, 1 M.C.O. saddle + one saddle G.S. - never any action taken in each case. The "Green line" having been captured Division is being relieved (for a short time probably) and is returning to the "Brown line".	many
"	11th		Sent more reserve stores to BLANGY DUMP. 1 Vickers Gun demanded for 112" M.G. Coy., there gun having been destroyed by shell fire. 1 interview with D.A.D.O.S. 12th Division.	many

WAR DIARY
or
INTELLIGENCE SUMMARY.
(Erase heading not required.)

Army Form C. 2118.

Place	Date	Hour	Summary of Events and Information	Remarks and references to Appendices
AGNES les DUISANS	12th		Division being withdrawn from the line. Informed by "Q" that Division will move back into "refill". The XVIII Corps is refitting out on schedule for "refilling". Renewed suspension of issues.	? Appx
"	13th		Informed ADOS XVIII Corps at HAUTEVILLE. ADOS VI Corps called. Preparations for move. Released and advanced dump at ARRAS of all stores re-issued - handed over remainder to relieving Division. Division moves to LIGNEREUIL area on the morrow - Whitsuntide AA + QMG. Orders for the move.	any
LIGNEREUIL	14th		Learnt that Division will probably have 7 days only before going into action again. Moved office, stores + shops to LIGNEREUIL. Wired 112th HY Bde to send in at once heavy guns for overhaul. Interviewed AA + QMG.	my
"	15th		To G.a.d.a. + Gun Park PREVENT to collect Lewis and Vickers Guns, unfired (to replace casualties in the Battle of ARRAS) - visited Heavy Mobile Workshop also. It being impossible to overhaul all the Lewis + Vickers Guns of the Division in the limited time at disposal, such 3 Ammunition SAA S,t,S,1,5 as advisable to overhaul machine Lewis guns with, instructions were to send in to Divl Armourers Shop all guns that themselves cannot be repaired by them.	my

WAR DIARY
or
INTELLIGENCE SUMMARY.
(Erase heading not required.)

Army Form C. 2118.

Place	Date	Hour	Summary of Events and Information	Remarks and references to Appendices
LIGNEREUIL	16th		Refitting — Heavy demands for Lewis guns (destroyed in recent operations). A.D.O.S. XVIII Corps called — ensured new supply. (Yesterday) — obtained from AA and QS authority to obtain 1000 suits of S.D. Clothing from Gen Park PREVENT. Trial of "Anti-aircraft portable mounting for Lewis guns" to "Q" Conference. To 10th. No. 11 Medium Workshop at GRAND RULLECOURT with A.A.Q.M.G. Workshop only just arrived — was without material. Obtained material from DDOS Third Army for manufacture of 16 Anti-aircraft portable mountings by Heavy Mobile Workshops PREVENT. At 8th Div 32 Lewis guns have been demanded & none is in place since destroyed. Railhead changes to TINQUES today.	✓
"	17th		Railhead TINQUES visited. It became for some time of reasonable stores. Total of Lewis guns destroyed than now reached 45. Summarised harassed losses in recent operations. Interviewed Divisional Baths Officer. Head Quarters 15 interviews AA+QMG.	✓
"	18th		Drew 12 Lewis guns complete from Gen Park PREVENT. T. AUBIGNY to 55 R.O.D. TINQUES — Arranged with return from trucks to be available for the return of worn clothing. Information by "Q" that Division will	

Army Form C. 2118.

WAR DIARY
or
INTELLIGENCE SUMMARY.
(Erase heading not required.)

Place	Date	Hour	Summary of Events and Information	Remarks and references to Appendices
LIGNEREUIL	18th		Move to XVII Corps in the morning - Head Quarters will move the day after. Interview with A.A.+Q.M.G.	—
"	19th		ADOS XVIII Corps called - explained that the troops made in refilling the Division. Obtained authority to draw 500 pairs of ankle boots from O.O. XVIII Corps Troops HAUTEVILLE.	—
"	20th		Division move to ETRUN tomorrow. Sent Stone to ETRUN and brought back stores of 4 Division Ordnance (both whom dump's and being salvaged), 4 Division advance doing likewise. Visits SEe + shops of DADOS. 4 Division at ETRUN and made arrangement for taking over in the morning. Borrowed 400 small box respirators from 4 Division to meet the immediate needs of reinforcements arriving without them. 63rd Inf Bde moved into the line and 111th Inf Bde into reserve trenches - taking over the front from the 4th Division. Collected 32 Lewis guns from 9th Bn PREVENT and issued 15 units from Main Divisional Dump ST NICHOLAS, ARRAS.	—
ETRUN	21st		Moved remainder of stores to ETRUN. Opened office at ETRUN infantry corps and army. Settling down - matters	—

Army Form C. 2118.

A 5834 Wt.W4973/M687 750,000 8/16 D.D. & L. Ltd. Forms/C.2118/13.

WAR DIARY or INTELLIGENCE SUMMARY

Army Form C. 2118.

Place	Date	Hour	Summary of Events and Information	Remarks and references to Appendices
ETRUN	Cont:- 21st		General arrangements from the accumulation of stores, shops and personnel. Collected Machine Gun Ammunition Belts (250 rounds) Collected 500 Lewis Gun Magazines from 6pm Park FREVENT also 5 No. 200 3rd Class C Wheels from Heavy Mobile Workshops with the same convoy. To Divisional Head Quarters (Rear Schelin).	nos/
"	22nd		Collected 1500 Magazines Lewis Gun from Gun Park, 10 Pistols Signalling 1" inch from Ordnance XVII Corps Troops AUBIGNY and sent them to Main Divisional Dump at ST. NICHOLAS, ARRAS. A Warrant Officer sent to Main Divisional Dump to supervise issue of Ordnance Stores, ie. lantern lamps, Black and Yellow Flags, Lewis Gun Ship's, sent to Dump. 11 P.M. Railhead changed to ARRAS.	m/
"	23rd		Attack started 4.45 a.m. Sent Divisional Reserves to ST. NICHOLAS Dump. ARRAS. Collected more "Parcels" being from Salvage dump and issued to Brigades. Through Ivanovar Officer or Main Divisional Dump. Refilled to 6 thru from Army Park whether notifiable by none of the depends of trucks from the Base	

Army Form C. 2118.

WAR DIARY
or
INTELLIGENCE SUMMARY.
(Erase heading not required.)

Place	Date	Hour	Summary of Events and Information	Remarks and references to Appendices
ETRUN	23rd	cont.	is essential. Reillhaud changes to GRANDE PLACE, ARRAS known.	—
"	24th	"	Advanced Head Quarters reported shortage of Vickers Gun Belts and Belt Boxes. Authority obtained to draw from FREVENT 5 un PARIS, 200 Belts and 50 Boxes. — collected these and issued through Main Divisional Dump according to allocation by "Q". To Advanced Head Quarters — returned AA 1919 on Entrance system relating to the afternoon. There afternoons is to be a great wastage of Belts, Ammunition and Magazines of Vickers Guns and Lewis Guns respectively. — Visited Very also are difficult to keep up to strength. Arranged with Divisional Railways Officer for 2 Armourers to be attached to him for quick overhaul of Vickers Belts, Lewis Gun Magazines &c so that they can be re-issued with little delay.	—
"	25th.		To AUBIGNY to see ADOS XVII Corps. — Pontoon wagon at 154 Coy RE destroyed by Shell fire — one to replace demanded from Base	

Army Form C. 2118.

WAR DIARY
or
INTELLIGENCE SUMMARY.
(Erase heading not required.)

Instructions regarding War Diaries and Intelligence Summaries are contained in F. S. Regs., Part II. and the Staff Manual respectively. Title pages will be prepared in manuscript.

Place	Date	Hour	Summary of Events and Information	Remarks and references to Appendices
ETRUN	25th cont.		by wire. Received to Railhead Lewis Gun Hopkinsons returned & were conspicuous by the issue of another Lewis Gun 9.S. per Battalion from the carriage of Lewis Gun Reformation to move in the morning.	m/
ARRAS	26th	11	To ARRAS — arranging accommodation for Stores Office, Shops and Personnel. Moved the whole outfit — BARRAS — settling down in new Quarters. Visited Main Dumps in & Dumps at ST NICHOLAS.	m/
"	"		Notified Corps and Army of new position. Signalling flags and Wire cables required, no items of manufacture of the former and returns of the Latter from various Salvage Dumps in ARRAS. Interviews with D.A.D.O.S. 9th Div. who will probably take over from me in a few days. 18th Cavalry demanded from Gun Park from A/51 Bde AFA — confirmed by 10th MAREUIL. Done Gun Carriage 15th from Gun Park. To PREVENT it	m/

WAR DIARY
or
INTELLIGENCE SUMMARY.

Army Form C. 2118.

Place	Date	Hour	Summary of Events and Information	Remarks and references to Appendices
ARRAS	28th cont		Visit Ordnance Heavy Mobile Workshops. Preparation for the return of surplus Brandts from Cavalry Divisions made. Div's will probably be withdrawn from the line in the next day or so. — Withdrawal commences tomorrow.	ms
"	29		Visited Wewent Officer in charge of Ordnance Stores at ST NICHOLAS Dump. Withdrawn probably handed over by 4th Divisions said it to Ordnance Officer XVII Corps Troops. Arrangements for moving to LIGNEREUIL tomorrow. Returned to Base Blundell's and KR's surplus owing to casualties. To LIGNEREUIL arranged with DADOS 4th Division to take over the saw-mill occupied by him. — Lorries loaded overnight.	ms
LIGNEREUIL	30th		Lorries left at 6 am for LIGNEREUIL. Returned Girl Salvage Dump of stores required for re-issue. Received Ordnance Branch at ST. NICHOLAS, ARRAS. Opened Office and Dump at LIGNEREUIL at 9 am. — informed DADOS Third Army DDOS XVIII Corps ADOS, and all units of Office + Dump Position.	ms

SECRET

37th Division.

War Diary for month ending 31st May, 1917.

37th Division.
3rd June, 1917

[signature]
D.A.D.V.O.S. Capt.,

WAR DIARY or INTELLIGENCE SUMMARY

Army Form C. 2118.

Place	Date	Hour	Summary of Events and Information	Remarks and references to Appendices
LIGNEREUIL	1st		Visited A.D.O.S XVIII Corps to gain information on 1st (motorable) shipment. Ammunition wagons are not motorable of stores & transport. Manual motor work in full swing.	m
"	2nd		Conference of Quartermasts (and Representative Officers of unit) Quartermasters & gun instructors with me said to the refitting of the Division, also to bring to notice various points affecting economy in material & equipment. A.D.O.S XVIII Corps assisted with same. Units have now received various important differences — 51 Lewis Gun tools & shell fins in action — demanded these from Gun Parts PREVENT.	m
"	3rd		Units commenced to relieve Wilbie Clothing. Sent 2 Armourer Staff Sgts to each Infr Bde to overhaul Lewis Gun Machine Gun arms generally. Surveyed finished losses in recent operations and submitted same to Base, Railhead damage of TINQUES. Demanded 1 Sikh 3 Italian gun (63 & 7th RB)17 - said to have been sent to Fifth Army School and lately thence to 63rd T.M.By asked for further information.	m
"	4th		Gradually Lewis & Vickers Guns in Inft Armourers Shop (those beyond repair of Armourers with Brigade). Work available.	m

Army Form C. 2118.

WAR DIARY
or
INTELLIGENCE SUMMARY.
(Erase heading not required.)

Instructions regarding War Diaries and Intelligence Summaries are contained in F.S. Regs., Part II. and the Staff Manual respectively. Title pages will be prepared in manuscript.

Place	Date	Hour	Summary of Events and Information	Remarks and references to Appendices
LIGNEREUIL	5th		Inspected with OC. Div. Train and ADVS the Transport of the 3 Field Ambulances. A.D.O.S. XVIII Corps ordered - amount to draw from OC. XVIII Corps Troops. The Book establishment is - 750 pairs. To Divisional Head Quarters. Completed output. Arrangement made is Commenced Payment to Base.	MTI
"	6th		Interviews with A.A. & Q.M.G. & D.D.O.S. Third Army. D.D.O.S. furnished visited Stores, huts and office. To TINQUES to visit R.O.D. called at THIRD ARMY GUN PARK IF FREVENT to collect Vickers gun and to enquire re outstanding demands. Divisional Head Quarters	m
"	7th		Visited 13th Rifle Bde to inspect Harness and Saddlery. Capt Belliot and Lt Chapman / Q'learners were instructed in the Definition generally in a Division. Divisional Head Quarters. Staff Montin received and receipts refunded in usual manner.	my
"	8th		Interviewed OC. Div Depot at FREVENT re provision of equipment for reinforcements. - nothing else of unusual importance.	my
"	9th		Made a thorough inspection of Divisional Armourers Shop. Divisional Transport Inspection. A.D.O.S. XVIII Corps called - obtained authority to draw 800 Jackets S.D. and 900 Trousers S.D. from XVIII Corps Troops.	my

Army Form C. 2118.

WAR DIARY
or
INTELLIGENCE SUMMARY.
(Erase heading not required.)

Place	Date	Hour	Summary of Events and Information	Remarks and references to Appendices
LIGNEREUIL	9th	cont.	Authority received from Corps to draw 200 Cups for Firing Rifle Grenades from Third Army Advance Gun Park. Divisional Hand Grenades.	—
"	10th	"	12 German Rifles drawn from BEAUMETZ Railhead on 3rd Army authority. 3 Trucks cleared at Railhead. 111th Bde Advance Wananer-officer accompanied Co. Due Train in connection of 111th bfts de transport.	—
"	11th	"	Collected 200 Cups, Rifle Grenade from 12th Army R.E. Workshops BETHUNE. Enquired at Third Army Gun Park re. outstanding demands. 3" Stokes Mortar received for 63rd T.M.Bty. Discussed with A.A. & Q.M.G. Advance Stores required from a Main Divisional Dump also what equipment is desirable to withdraw from action.	—
"	12th	"	Gunwheeled German Machine Guns recently captured. Conference to decide best form of super structure for carrying supply bolted tins on MK Y Cart Watertank. Interview A.A. & Q.M.G.	—
"	13th	"	Nothing of unusual importance.	—
"	14th	"	Collected from GUNPARK, FREVENT various Lewis Gun Parts. Made enquiries of at No 11 Medium Gunware Workshops, GRANDE contd.	—

WAR DIARY
or
INTELLIGENCE SUMMARY.
(Erase heading not required.)

Army Form C. 2118.

Place	Date	Hour	Summary of Events and Information	Remarks and references to Appendices
LIGNEREUIL	14th cont-		RULLECOURT in order to find out whether retirs & vehicles are to be sent out quickly - probably Division will be in "ant" march much longer. Informed by Q that division will probably move on 18th instant -	ms
"	15th		Interview A.D.O.S. XVIII Corps re. hastening issue of Hotch-kiss Magazines and Spare Parts, Match Lewis Gun Slings, and Blacksmith & forge in Div Shops to complete Divn in establishment. Head Quadn in company Armourer Staff Sergeant Guilavan given acty command of Warrant Officers and was placed in charge of Divl Armourer's Shop.	ms
"	16th		2,500 Lewis Gun Magazines, 20 Bags Shrapnel, & S.C. Relot and 4th Vickers Gun Belts Ammunition due to this formation drawn from Gun Park FREVENT. Barrel of 3" Stokes Mortar damaged beyond repair during practice firing - demanded and replaced by new. To ARRAS 15 am any "taking over" from D.A.D.O.S. 56th Divn.	ms
"	17th		Railhead becomes ARRAS on the 19th instant. Division to have	ms

A 8534 Wt W4973/M687 750,000 8/16 D. D. & L. Ltd. Forms/C.2118/13.

WAR DIARY
or
INTELLIGENCE SUMMARY.
(Erase heading not required.)

Army Form C. 2118.

Place	Date	Hour	Summary of Events and Information	Remarks and references to Appendices
LIGNEREUIL	17th	6 p.m.	On march 18th-19th instant DADOS 2nd Division came to arrange taking over. Divl Head Quarters.	nil
"	18th	"	Preparations for the move to WARLUS tomorrow. Manual vehicles away	nil
WARLUS	19th	"	Railhead near ARRAS. Moved Office, Stores, Shops and Personnel to WARLUS commencing 6 a.m. Divisional Head Quarters	nil
"	20th	"	Visited DADOS 56th Divn. at ARRAS to make final arrangements for taking over. – Called on ADOS VI Corps on return journey. Collected 3, 15/h Q.F. Guns from Gun Parks PREVENT and issued them to 10th VI Corps ARRAS. 17th and 33rd Divl Artillery transferred to me from Ordnance Advance Administrative DADOS 12 Divs.	nil
ARRAS	21st	"	Transferred Office, Stores Shops and Personnel to ARRAS No 42 Rue D'AMIENS. Amusing accommodation. – Divl Hd. Quarters	nil
"	22nd	"	Discussed with DADOS 12th Divn. various points arising from transfer of 17th + 33rd Divl Artilleries. – Settling down generally in new Quarters.	nil
"	23rd	"	Interview with O/c Third Army Gun Park – Nothing else of unusual	nil

Army Form C. 2118.

WAR DIARY
or
INTELLIGENCE SUMMARY.
(Erase heading not required.)

Place	Date	Hour	Summary of Events and Information	Remarks and references to Appendices
ARRAS	23rd	cont	...importance.	—
"	24		Dis engaged with 10th VI Corps Light Workshop present position refitting 5m tanks with special reference to spares. Lieut K/DAC, 18th gm. Only demanded for C/156 Bde RFA is replace one condemned by I.O.M. 2 Watercarts and 1 Wagon limbered GS demanded to replace vehicles condemned by I.O.M. List of Artillery m/s advance sent to CAFAIS - demands for stores in Sections 14-15 less 16B Survey to be sent to Nouvelle base after much M- 27/28 m'sheet. To Heavy Mobile Workshop FREVENT. 11 Lewis Guns collected from Gen Park - Division is now complete with Lewis gun. Inspected Head of Quarries	—
"	26th		AA & QMG and self visited Corps Ammunition Shop in Rue de Lille ARRAS. - then to 111th Bde Head Quarters. TILLOY en MOFFLAINES. Usual bathing and disinfecting arrangements for "Q".	—
"	27th		Nothing of unusual importance.	—

WAR DIARY or INTELLIGENCE SUMMARY

Army Form C. 2118.

Place	Date	Hour	Summary of Events and Information	Remarks and references to Appendices
ARRAS	28th		18 fur Gun any demanded for A/19 Bde. Instructions enclosed by L.O.M. for Scouring. Div. Head Quarters.	—
"	29th		Division will be relieved on June 2nd 10am by 61st Division. — all attached units will cease to be employed as there — Instructions issue to all except attached units. Preparations for moving 17th Bhds. to withdrawn from all Troops and sent to Base. Interviewed DADOS 61st Div. re handing over. Div. Head Quarters.	—
"	30th		Transferred units attached temporarily to this Division to DADOS 61st — Bures notified by wire — others (Corps Army, Division, 10M VII Corps) will be sent ORLS on morning of June 1st. Instructed 9/15th carriage and 4/5 hour/p. away from 5pm onwards FRESENT and handed them over to I.O.M VI Corps — Notified receipt in usual manner. Informed to AA.QMG. That Division moves to LIGNEREUIL area on the 2nd June — D.H.Q. opens (at 10 am that date. DADOS 61st called to arrange final details of taking over V.S. Lea DADOS 3rd Div. at LIGNEREUIL to arrange taking over of his office about 3.E.C. Divisional Head Quarters.	—
"	31st			—

31-5-17
[signature]
DADOS 37 Div

37th Division.

War Diary for month ending 30th June, 1917.

John H Hopcroft
D.A.D.V.S. Capt.

Army Form C. 2118.

WAR DIARY
or
INTELLIGENCE SUMMARY.
(Erase heading not required.)

Instructions regarding War Diaries and Intelligence Summaries are contained in F. S. Regs., Part II. and the Staff Manual respectively. Title pages will be prepared in manuscript.

Place	Date	Hour	Summary of Events and Information	Remarks and references to Appendices
ARRAS	1st	7am	Arrangements for moving to LIGNEREVIL in progress.	—
LIGNEREVIL	2nd	"	Moved Office, Stores & Staff to LIGNEREVIL. Railhead changed to TINQUES. Handed over our Dump ARRAS to DADOS 61st Div. the stores for attached units.	nil
"	3rd	"	Collected Lewis Gun Parts from Third Army Gun Park. 175 sets of Packsaddlery issued to this Division for officers in Artillery withdrawn from units and handed over to DADOS 61st Div. Division in XVIII Corps from today inclusive. Jnd. Head Quarters	—
"	4th	"	Nothing of unusual importance.	—
"	5th	"	List of units sent to CALAIS with request that issue of stores be resumed. Division will be in First Army from 6th instant inclusive.	—
"	6th	"	To BOMY 10 am and accommodation for advance Detachment in new AREA. Jnd. Head Quarters.	—
"	7th	"	4 Lorries to BOMY at 5AM – two men left in charge. Cleaning and arranging moved Summary. Transferred of [illegible]	—

Army Form C. 2118.

WAR DIARY
or
INTELLIGENCE SUMMARY.
(Erase heading not required.)

Instructions regarding War Diaries and Intelligence Summaries are contained in F. S. Regs., Part II. and the Staff Manual respectively. Title pages will be prepared in manuscript.

Place	Date	Hour	Summary of Events and Information	Remarks and references to Appendices
LIQUERCUIL	7th		ordinary demands in Gun Park Third Army to Gun Park First Army. - Railhead LILLERS.	my
ROMY	8th		Moved detachment, office, dump and stores to ROMY.	my
"	9th		To First Army Hd Qrs LILLERS - then to following Gun Park BRUAY. Arranging accommodation etc generally, no new location.	my
"	10th		Interviews A.D. + Q.M.G. re Distinguished Patches - Nothing else of manual importance.	my
"	11th		To D.D.O.S First Army LILLERS - thence to MERVILLE and LA GORGUE re ammunition repair of vehicles. Inducts for 37 Div Artillery handed over by DADOS 21st Div. Dist Head of Quarters.	my
"	12th		2 Armourers S+S,S sent to each Brigade for duty. Routine work.	my
"	13th		Nothing of unusual importance.	my
"	14th		C.I.O.M. First Army called and inspected mine vehicles in zone of repair respectively. Representative of 3 Infantry Bgden met and discussed possibilities -	my

A.5834 Wt. W4973/M687 750,000 8/16 D. D. & L. Ltd. Forms/C.2118/13

Army Form C. 2118.

WAR DIARY
or
INTELLIGENCE SUMMARY.
(Erase heading not required.)

Place	Date	Hour	Summary of Events and Information	Remarks and references to Appendices
BOMY	14		Anti-aircraft Lewis gun mount made in Div¹ Armourer's Shop.	
	15		Taking over from Capt. MENZIES DADOS who proceeds on leave; going over work & getting papers in order; SGM inspecting billets.	
	16		C.I.O.M. First Army trying to find me; many 25 infantry various vehicles complaints as his inspection arranged; Interview with N.C.O. I/C mice 25 northern LIMBERS; all Louis guns repaired to be re-issued; 112 Bde. G guns would be repaired but units must take in 360.	
	17		Visit to "A" Echelon DAC chief complaining vehicles whilst a/E supply Transport harness; Sending 68 Bde. 10 extra Lewis Guns adapted for use at a sling; spare for 112 Bde.; machines with "G" scale of all requisite needs for 20000 Armourer Sh.	
	18		Visit to 63 Bde. FORGES discussing cartridges funnels; and pulley terminology ending up entry 300 salt being enroute to work of Lithain; saw another Mail hop; SGM now busy behind and setting up for the Division.	
	19		FIRST ARMY training Establishment of 2nd Army recently been & applying distribution; went to 112 Bde. interview NCO I/C tracing out things through SGM and Kadela that was his fault I Cal amount 400 before suitable; Saturday DADO, busy in hypostating mine of Second ARMY of ammunition w Bethune; Saturday ARMY of amm w SETHUNE; could kindly advised to frame articles 20 miles of some of SERD; arranging to hire firm made up at one continuous in Estree storing; army of DDOS to handing lorry back at Estree; not wanted; know C.I.O.M's inspection to be continued & reported beyond reply; if Aerodrome nr. C.I.O.M's Armourer Sh? arranged to see in bring Div. village from the MONS; to Armourer work any Corps PRESENT to release Bde. Armr. Companies return to this immensely troubled situation; ambulance 5M LI and also 65 towns from each other apart immediately; while G. STEEN BECQUE wraps DHP roams to within 23 Y on LG CAPETRE another staying over; interviewing G. SABEL Second army HTP arranged to overhaul lorry & CASSTAS another	
	20		arranging in ambulance in each time of reported to C.I.OM'n now, to note the BOS FIRST ARMY, arranging to hand over 32 SD waiting Armourer to refurbishes 25 Sers who could come in from 2 ft.; many C.I.O.M has now also been employed refining today. 1 to see my Every man for Paris to Cours; in times enquires, Armoury more tell on best in steps under to the be retained. Some also; Suddenly Interview along Secy to 20. III Army Corps PREVENT.	
	21			
	22		Capt. appl². heavy arms smith; everyone sunny day 1 GOOD bi-weekly Trip made up at II Army RE inspecting; training manual rev. C.I.O.M. First Army; interview with DADOS 25 Drs?; arranging for his hire on 23 & & 24th; while at GRANDURE and Guns at Hq/J Armoury ammunition for moon. Wire received at 10h 30 hours 30-0-18.	

WAR DIARY or INTELLIGENCE SUMMARY

Army Form C. 2118.

Place	Date	Hour	Summary of Events and Information	Remarks and references to Appendices
STEENBECQUE	23		Steppy & party of 5 and officers to DRANOUTRE: proceeding there and staying from DHQ & offices proceeding by 11.15 train; train to 36 Div'n subsequently to ADMS (Col WALKER) IX Corps superintg. & his appt'm. proposed subject to confirmation by our R.I. primarily Divs at STEENWOORDE & superintg. Remainder of O.Rs & officers move from BOMY to DRANOUTRE, mostly Belm. in motor lorries via CALSTRE, THIENNES, BLETS OF LOCRE. Enroute parties up coaches & assigning stores moving CALAIS via Comd'l. Summer stand 26°.	Apx 5
DRANOUTRE	24		Visiting DHQ & 15 army specialist installations: calls from DMS & 36 Divs also running & inspections of various points which are hard to unload will be open for these kinds to fall. S.I. Forge & Barnes have by army's inspectly stone shops opened. Entering over 18 compl[ete] & workmate'l. being from 11 Divs: working 30 wkd westn of TARUA.	Apx 5
	25		Radiations from Invalid Park showed fair Guns have not arrived. Meanwhile 18 Div'n Conners had three church horses; office being informated in camp. Visit of TADS IX Corps & RPO informed that an ophonh'wtng & Gun Park etc must move off-day improvements in Lamps, large sign installed for Pte T. Sheriff brought into his leapline hosp. & an meanwhile Ord Dept's stores temporarily at Boy H.F. & 112 on beside; sumps being installed by Plant to store hospitals.	Apx 5
	26		Adm. Mp ? 12 invitn. to 63 Fd Amb H.Q. & Amy: intend of these had onlies as at approve of timber pieces.	
	27		Took over from 1st Taylm one motor lorries & two cars. Inspects'n with stores shops and offices and onwards.	
			AD + QMG at D.H.Q.	
	28		Discussed transfer of misc'l from 36" & 37 Div'n with DADOS 36" & 37 yrs. (calling about m.d. tillage in the area. Division'l Head Quartis arrive from LOCRE to DRANOUTRE on the 11th. Interview ADOS IX Corps who visited store shops and offices. Army journey to for the relief of men.	
	29		Divisional Head Quarters — Duties and front is being considerably reduced, but–functions of Ordnance Dept will be still sufficiently continue.	

WAR DIARY
INTELLIGENCE SUMMARY

Place	Date	Hour	Summary of Events and Information	Remarks and references to Appendices
BRANDHOEK	30		To 2nd Army R.E. Workshops HAZEBROUCK. Collect and return indents for "Q". A.O.O.S Second Army called. Nothing unusual to report.	

John M Ingoals
Capt
DADOS
37 Div.

30—6—17.

SECRET.

37th Division.

War Diary for month ended 31st July, 1917.

3/8/1917

John H. Horrocks
Capt.,
D.A.D.O.S., 37th Division.

WAR DIARY
or
INTELLIGENCE SUMMARY.

Army Form C. 2118.

(Erase heading not required.)

Place	Date	Hour	Summary of Events and Information	Remarks and references to Appendices
BRANDOUTRE	1st July		Visited Railhead HAEGEDOORNE and BRULOOZE. Railhead changes to BRULOOZE tomorrow. Nothing else of moment to report.	
"	2nd "		To Second Army School of Sniping in the morning — then to Second Army RE Workshops HAZEBROUCK to collect Anti-Aircraft Mountings for Machine Guns.	
"	3rd "		Commenced re-inoculation of all men who have not been inoculated for 12 months — received notification that BATT HQS. the end of day. To Second Army for Route to Infantry tactical schemes of attack apparently demand up to knowledge of use of Lewis 14" Gun Artillery will shortly be allotted A.S. to me from G Armee. amendments also	
"	4th "		61, 62 and 89 Fd Coys RE and 11th Kings battalion Coronation Bath will be attached (temporarily) G.d Head Quarters.	
"	5th "		Summary through arrival of all Bringle in the Division. Nothing else of moment on [?].	

WAR DIARY
or
INTELLIGENCE SUMMARY.
(Erase heading not required.)

Army Form C. 2118.

Place	Date	Hour	Summary of Events and Information	Remarks and references to Appendices
DRANOUTRE	6th		14th Divisional Artillery transferred from by DADOS, 50 Div. — 37 Div. Artillery transferred by CO. 37 Div. to 14 Corps. Railhead changed to HAEGEDOORNE with ADOS IX Corps. Tomorrow. Command assumed by Anon Staff Sgt, of all bicycles in the Division.	
"	7th		Ssk of all bicycles in the Division — Divisional provision of Anti-aircraft Machine gun Mountings with AA & QMG. To Second Army Heavy Mobile Workshop to obtain full chain for Shrouder tones in exchange for empty — interview with D.D.O.S. Seen a barge in CASSEL. 76th Sanitary Section transferred to me from 36th Div. Divisional Head Quarters	
"	8/8		37th Div. Artillery relieves 14th Divl Arty during night of 9th-10th. — 14 Divl Artillery will be transferred to Armour Administrative L DADOS, 14th Div, when 14 Divr arrives in IX Corps. Nothing else of unusual importance	
"	9th		Usual Administrative work — Divisional Head Quarters	
"	10th		To Second Army R.E. Workshop in Anti Aircraft Sights —	

WAR DIARY or INTELLIGENCE SUMMARY

Army Form C. 2118.

Place	Date	Hour	Summary of Events and Information	Remarks and references to Appendices
DRANOUTRE	10th cont		Them to Heavy Ordnance Workshops to exchange empty Shrapnel cases for duds. Divisional Head Quarters.	ms
"	11th		Interviewed Staff Captain 37 Div Artillery on various matters – given authy to find carts for his (collected) Artillery with regard to move out all cart-stores. Inspected munition ammunition Columns (to complete to Second Army Scale) from O.O. Army Troops Sub. Depot at CAESTRE. Ascertained position of Divisional Bomb Carriers of various types and demands in respect of deficiencies in bulk	ms
"	12th		Moved office into Head Quarters Camp. Interviewed DADOS 14th Divn - demand not to transfer to him until in hand with me until situation in Eastern Prov. known. Divisional Head Qrs.	ms
"	13th		Demanded Hoof Pincer enclosures to wire – (authority given by Second Army for 8 & 3). Issued Caution in Artilly. Nothing else of unusual importance.	ms

WAR DIARY
or
INTELLIGENCE SUMMARY.
(Erase heading not required.)

Army Form C. 2118.

Place	Date	Hour	Summary of Events and Information	Remarks and references to Appendices
DRANOUTRE	14th		Transferred all units of 19th Div. attached to 34 Div for administration to DADOS 19 Div. Carried out the further "dispersion stops" to the Tripods of 111th M.G. Coy. Discussed with Staff Capt. R.A. 39th Divy. outstanding demands from 59m. Divisional Head Quarters.	✓
"	15th		Visited ADOS IX Corps chiefly about transfer of Artillery and ordinary demands on the 59m. Interviewed D.O.T.M. to decide method in which rounds should be submitted for Bulk and Detail Shown by Trench Mortar Batteries.	✓
"	16th		Carrying out and inspection of Bicycles on charge to Divl. Artillery. A.D.O.S. IX Corps called & inspected office stone schedules. Drew arms & ammunition unit detachment of "Q" and DADOS. Divl. Head Quarters.	✓
"	17th		Arranged for 4 men (1 from each Bahn) of 63rd Inf Bde to be attached to Divl Armourer's Shop for a 10 days course of instruction. Visited 2nd Army R.E. and Ordnance Workshop with AA&QMG	✓

WAR DIARY or INTELLIGENCE SUMMARY

Army Form C. 2118.

Place	Date	Hour	Summary of Events and Information	Remarks and references to Appendices
DRANOUTRE	18th		D.D.O.S Second Army visited Store and Shops. Attended demonstration of the use of the "Yukon Pack" — given by Captain Dunwalters. Manual sentries useful.	m
"	19h		Visited Captain Dunwalters at Second Army Smithy School to obtain information as to improvements to the type of "Yukon Pack" at present issued by the Base. — afterwards to Second Army R.E. and Ordnance Workshops. Arrangements to supply out- alteration to all Yukon Packs in the Division. Divisional Head Quarters	m
"	20th		No. 247 (Div) M. Gun Coy joined the division from England. Base notified. Nothing else of unusual importance.	m
"	21st		Trial of standard metal brazier. Inspection of 247 M.G. Coy to ascertain any important differences. Lewis Gun belongings to 8" E. Lancs discharged by shell fire — (ammunition) no replace by wire.) Inspection of all Bicycles in the Division completed. Answered from guns of 247 M.G. Coy to the overhauled by Armourers from Div. Shops. St. Sgt Toyra reported from training as a Bde. W.O.	m
"	22nd		St Sgt Toyre ordered to join O.O. XIV Corps. for duty. Nothing else	m

A.5834 Wt W4973/M687 750,000 8/16 D. D. & L. Ltd. Forms/C.2118/13.

Army Form C. 2118.

WAR DIARY
or
INTELLIGENCE SUMMARY.
(Erase heading not required.)

Instructions regarding War Diaries and Intelligence Summaries are contained in F.S. Regs., Part II. and the Staff Manual respectively. Title pages will be prepared in manuscript.

Place	Date	Hour	Summary of Events and Information	Remarks and references to Appendices
DRANOUTRE	22nd		of unusual importance.	—
"	23rd		S/Sgt Toyce left for D.O.S. Steenwerck with instructions from D.O.S. Steenwerck with improved pack-saddles. Informing design of portable Lewis Gun Mounting. Demanded by wire a MK IV Tripod for Vickers gun to replace one destroyed by shell fire. Drawins Hot Gun on various subjects. 80 Hot fennel containers received from the Base.	we
"	24th		Collected 6 attitudes and 7 anti aircraft sights from R.E. Workshops HAZEBROUCK. 80 Hot fennel containers received from the Base. Visited ADOS IX Corps to arrange supply of special stores for unit of division. Interview with OADOS 14 Div re depression in guns of 14th Div Arty. Divisional Head Quarters.	—
"	25th		17 Handcarts received from the Base for infantry: — 140 Julum Packs and 2 Walla Carts (with harness) drawn from OTO IX Corps Troops for same purpose. 18m cannage demanded by wire for 123rd Bde RFA to replace one destroyed by shell fire received by 10.7.	—

WAR DIARY or INTELLIGENCE SUMMARY

Army Form C. 2118.

Place	Date	Hour	Summary of Events and Information	Remarks and references to Appendices
BRANDHOEK	26th		4.5 Howitzers received from the Base for D/123 Bde RFA. Nothing else of mutual information.	my
"	27th		Arranged with 10M. IX Corps, for the refair of 5 limited R.E. Wagons taking to Signal Coy. – parts being unobtainable from the Base – Usual routine work.	my
"	28th		To La MOTTE au BOIS. 15 arrange with Front Control for the supply of 3000 stones for use with Yukon Packs. Journeyed from Base by mine a Vickers Gun Complete to refilace one belonging to 112 M.G. Coy. destroyed by shell fire. 20000 waterproof sheets received from O.O. IX Corps. to be issued. Thu 16 63rd Inf Bde for commn. of winter. Divisional Head Quarters. Usual routine work.	my
"	29th			my
"	30th		2 Q.F. 15pr guns received from Base for C/127 Bde RFA. 89 Special Penistokes (No 30) this received – these have to be trucked on Train at Stores. Sent Stores (300) from use with Yukon Packs, 15 63rd Bde Transport Lines by lorry.	my
"	31st		Attack commenced 3.50 A.M. 30 Hot food Containers sent to Corps.	my

Army Form C. 2118.

WAR DIARY
or
INTELLIGENCE SUMMARY.
(Erase heading not required.)

Place	Date	Hour	Summary of Events and Information	Remarks and references to Appendices
DRANOUTRE	31st contd		63rd Bde. - Despatch of 2 18 pr Q F carriages and 1 18pr Q F gun notified by the Base. Divl Head Quarters.	my
	31-7-17			

John H. Jacobs
Capt DADOS
37 Divn

SECRET

37th Division.

War Diary for month ending 31st August, 1917.

37th Division,
2nd Sept., 1917.

[signature]
Capt.,
D.A.D.O.S.

WAR DIARY
or
INTELLIGENCE SUMMARY.
(Erase heading not required.)

Army Form C. 2118.

Place	Date	Hour	Summary of Events and Information	Remarks and references to Appendices
DRANOUTRE	1st August		Two 18 pr QF carriages received for Divl Artillery — also one 18 pr QF Spre. Smith bore found out of order & sent to Brigade in the line & one — weather very bad. Arranged with ADOS for supply of Vickers barrels from Corps pool when required.	
"	2nd		2 18 pr QF carriages and 4 Lewis Guns demanded by wire from the base to replace those destroyed by enemy fire. Sent 52 Vickers Barrels and 250 Vickers Bdrs to M.G. Coys in the line these being urgently required to replace unserviceable. Original Head Quarter.	
"	3rd		Arranged with ADOS IX Corps for immediate supply of 2000 suits S.D. and 3000 prs of socks for issue to 63rd Inf Bde — just withdrawn from the line. Sent 4 Armourer S.S.Sy'ts with their assistants to 63rd Bde to overhaul all 15 weapons and Vickers Guns of 112th M.G. Coy in Divl Armourers Shop. Arranged and in possession of Battalions of Major-General.	
"	4th		2000 suits S.D. 3000 prs of socks and 3000 pairs of	

Army Form C. 2118.

WAR DIARY
or
INTELLIGENCE SUMMARY.
(Erase heading not required.)

Instructions regarding War Diaries and Intelligence Summaries are contained in F. S. Regs., Part II. and the Staff Manual respectively. Title pages will be prepared in manuscript.

Place	Date	Hour	Summary of Events and Information	Remarks and references to Appendices
DRANOUTRE	4th cont		Gun Boots received from CALAIS by lorry and distributed in accordance with "Q" instructions. — Three armourers went. Division many men on the 7 instant.	
"	5th		Demanded by wire a Vickers M.G. toolplace in destroyed. Interview with DADOS of Australian Division who will take over my present dump. Three armourers working.	
"	6th		To LOCRE and district to become acquainted with new area. Arrangements for movement to LOCRE on the 8. Provisional Head Quarters.	
"	7th		All Lewis Guns demanded arrived from Base — also one Vickers gun. Arrangements for move. Moved shops to LOCRE. Div. Head Quarters.	
LOCRE	8th		Established office/store shops at LOCRE. — searched all area for a more convenient location. Handed over various Trench & Area Stores to DADOS of Australian Division.	

A.834 Wt. W4973/M687 750,000 8/16 D.D.& L. Ltd. Forms/C.2118/13.

Army Form C. 2118.

WAR DIARY
or
INTELLIGENCE SUMMARY.
(Erase heading not required.)

Instructions regarding War Diaries and Intelligence Summaries are contained in F.S. Regs., Part II. and the Staff Manual respectively. Title pages will be prepared in manuscript.

Place	Date	Hour	Summary of Events and Information	Remarks and references to Appendices
LOCRE	9th		To A.D.O.S. IX Corps. — Then to 127th Capt 63rd Infantry Bde. Arranged for supply of fine appliances by 9th Battn. Interview with Staff Capt. 111 Inf Bde. re new type of L.G. cannon. aphaning its use. Jnd. Head Quarters.	
"	10th		ADOS IX Corps called + inspected office stone shops. — nothing else of unusual importance.	
"	11th		Usual routine work.	
"	12th		Railhead changed to BRULOOZE. 2 water carts received one for D/124 Bde RFA + other for B/124 Bde RFA. collected from 0.0 IX Div. Troops 600 pairs gum Boots Thigh for issue to 63rd Inf Bde. collected 1200 pairs gum Boots Thigh for issue was from CAESTRE. Issued 5 special Lewis Gun Slings to 63rd Inf Bde for trial purposes. Jnd. Head Quarters.	
"	13th		To Sec. ad. Army R.E. + Ordnance Workshops — re Anti Aircraft sights + fastenings for entrenching implements. Jnd. Head Quarters.	
"	14			

WAR DIARY or INTELLIGENCE SUMMARY

Army Form C. 2118.

Place	Date	Hour	Summary of Events and Information	Remarks and references to Appendices
LOCRE	15th		Usual routine work.	nil
"	16th		Bore hole for camp water received from the Base - stove and fire also received at behind time.	nil
"	17th		To HAZEBROUCK to collect Anti-Aircraft Sights & Fuses for Enemy Aircraft. Interviews with AA & QMS re Supply of Canvas. Retrieved damaged Telescopic Sights to Second Army Store of Sniping Posts & Cols - arranged supply of material for Telescopic Rifles for Divisions within Second Army.	nil
"	18th		Usual routine work.	nil
"	19th		Despatch of 2 Water-carts advised by the Base - this conflicts with instructions demands from units. Formerly supplied. The new type of water-cart - tried on walk-out superstructure. Divisional Head Quarters.	nil
"	20th		To BAILLEUL to great [Junction?]. Interview with AA & QMS re nature of clothing to Base, also re superstructure on Travelling Kitchens.	nil

Army Form C. 2118.

WAR DIARY
or
INTELLIGENCE SUMMARY.
(Erase heading not required.)

Instructions regarding War Diaries and Intelligence Summaries are contained in F. S. Regs., Part II. and the Staff Manual respectively. Title pages will be prepared in manuscript.

Place	Date	Hour	Summary of Events and Information	Remarks and references to Appendices
LOCRE	21st		Interviewed O.C. 112 MG Coy, also the Divisional Machine Gun Officer. 210 Rattles for Steel Gas alarms received from the Base. Issued 1600 Water Covers. Two amongst infantry Battn. Pioneers. Jos. Bond Qualities.	N
"	22nd		Moral Routine work.	N
"	23rd		To Second Army Workshops to collect stores manufactured for the Division. 2 Water Carts received from the Base - (for 0/123rd Bde & 0/124 Bde). Discussed revision Machine Gun question with the Divisional Machine Gun Officer.	N
"	24th		Visited 0/124 Bde RFA with Staff Capt Dunbar to inspect all wagon line equipment - heavy shortages have been reconstructed arrangements from Rhine mill Interview ADOS IX Corps also Lieut O & O or 19th Div. Pte Joslyn to be sent from Second Army Lt QM is refunded Pte Welsh being sent to the Base	N
"	25th		3 looks Goods to replace L.G.S. wagon received for the 3 field Coys; R.E. Interview with OMG is re optical sights for	N

Army Form C. 2118.

WAR DIARY
or
INTELLIGENCE SUMMARY.
(Erase heading not required.)

Instructions regarding War Diaries and Intelligence Summaries are contained in F. S. Regs., Part II. and the Staff Manual respectively. Title pages will be prepared in manuscript.

Place	Date	Hour	Summary of Events and Information	Remarks and references to Appendices
LOCRE	25th	cont.	Machine Guns. Sent suggestions re alteration of establishments of D.H.Q's + B.H.Q (Ordnance) to A.D.O.S.	my
"	26th		Usual routine work.	my
"	27th		Interview with D.A.Q.M.G. re: Gum Boots, Socks, Hatford (cookers) + shirts for winter. Nothing else of importance.	my
"	28th		Issued special form of Grenade Carrier to Battns for trial. Gum Boots issued to units according to "Q" allotment. Interview with A.A. & Q.M.G. re losses of equipment by artillery. Replied to letter from A.D.O.S. asking for suggestions re improvement of numerical S.O. clothing — present % being low.	my
"	29th		Drew in ×50 allotment of Hot food containers for use of the Brigade going into the line v the extended Divisional front.	my
"	30th		Nothing of unusual importance.	my

Army Form C. 2118.

WAR DIARY
or
INTELLIGENCE SUMMARY.
(Erase heading not required.)

Instructions regarding War Diaries and Intelligence Summaries are contained in F. S. Regs., Part II. and the Staff Manual respectively. Title pages will be prepared in manuscript.

Place	Date	Hour	Summary of Events and Information	Remarks and references to Appendices
LOCRE	31st	"	Issued tintage and showing material to 63rd Bde for accommodation in new area. Interviewed D.O.TTY. re demand for a 9.45 TTY. Sub-hd. — also discussed with him the Trench Mortar return. Arrangements issued for explanations to a Naval Party visiting the front.	note

31-8-17.

Johnny[?]Jants
Capt
DADOS
37 Div

SECRET

37th Division.

War Diary for month ending 30th September, 1917.

37th Division,
3rd October, 1917.

John H. Mowat
Capt.
D.A.D.O.S.

Army Form C. 2118.

WAR DIARY
or
INTELLIGENCE SUMMARY.
(Erase heading not required.)

Instructions regarding War Diaries and Intelligence Summaries are contained in F.S. Regs., Part II. and the Staff Manual respectively. Title pages will be prepared in manuscript.

Place	Date	Hour	Summary of Events and Information	Remarks and references to Appendices
LOCRE	Sept. 1st		To Heavy Mobile Workshops, to obtain spares for 6" Newton T.M's, and for refilling of Stokes Hows Air Spindles. Usual routine work.	nil
"	2nd		Nothing of unusual importance.	nil
"	3rd		Interview with Quartermaster of 10" RF and 13 KRRC. Issued new form of hiring (hypothecar?) for trial. Divl Head Qtrs. moved. Usual routine work. Sub Condr Mason, chief clerk went on leave to England.	nil
"	4th		Sub-let for 9.45 MK II Heavy Trench Mortars received from Base Reinforcement to D.O.T.M. 36th Div — the H.T.M. being shortage of total. 1 — 36th Div Arty. Divisional Heavy Quartil. (all did 14 oro pairs of Gum Boots Thigh from CAESTRE for issue to Bri'd in new area. Issued holding to Train Coys of 19" Div. travelled in our area.	nil
"	5th			nil
"	6th			nil
"	7th		Usual routine work.	nil
"	8th		To Railhead BRULOOZE — then 15 YORK HOUSE on the VIERSTRAAT road to inspect the Salvage Dump (forward). Ammunition conts.	nil

A.5834 Wt. W4973/M687 750,000 8/16 D. D. & L. Ltd. Forms/C.2118/13.

Army Form C. 2118.

WAR DIARY
or
INTELLIGENCE SUMMARY.
(Erase heading not required.)

Instructions regarding War Diaries and Intelligence Summaries are contained in F. S. Regs., Part II. and the Staff Manual respectively. Title pages will be prepared in manuscript.

Place	Date	Hour	Summary of Events and Information	Remarks and references to Appendices
LOCRE	8th	cont.	with DADOS 19th Div. the following over to his office Stores Etc at ST. JANS CAPPEL – commencing with DUC Shops and Reserves at 8 am on the 18th instar. D.D.O.S. Second Army called and inspected shops, stores and Office.	ms ✓
"	9th		Visited DADOS 19th Division for purpose of arranging accommodation for office, shops and Stores pertaining to Ordnance.	ms ✓
"	10th		Moved Armourers' Shop and Reserves to ST. JANS CAPPEL. Attended conference of DADSOS at ADOS. IX Corps' office MONT NOIR. Handed over Lyon Back Thigh Straps 19 Div. Arranged to move remaining Shops, Stores and Office to ST. JANS CAPPEL tomorrow. Divisional Head Quarters.	ms ✓
"	11th		Moved Stores and Office to ST. JANS CAPPEL. Interview with Staff Capt. R.A.	ms ✓
ST. JANS CAPPEL	12th		Railhead changed to HAGEDOORNE ~~BRULOOZE~~ – Corps and Army informed – Motor ground arrangements in new location.	ms ✓

WAR DIARY
or
INTELLIGENCE SUMMARY.
(Erase heading not required.)

Army Form C. 2118.

Place	Date	Hour	Summary of Events and Information	Remarks and references to Appendices
ST JANS CAPPELL	13th		To MERVILLE to draw Chaffcutters for A.D.O.S. Drew 10,500 Blankets from O.O. Second Army Troops at CAESTRE and issued them on a scale of 1 per man to all units of the Division. Divisional Head Quarters	cont.
"	14th		Visited ADOS IX Corps – also the Field Cashier to draw for payment. Divisional Head Quarters.	cont.
"	15th		Transferred 76 Sanitary Section to OO 17 Corps Troops. Visited DADOS 19th Divn. and O.C. 63rd TM Bty. Nothing else of unusual importance.	cont.
"	16th		To DUNKIRK to purchase "Kulet" weapons apparel from camouflage purposes. – Manual machine wrecked.	cont.
"	17th		Naval Routine work. – 9pm demanded (18lb, 6pm only) for A/124 Bde Guns.	cont.
"	18th		Sub. Condr. Hann, chief clerk returned from leave. Collected 2,000 Blankets from CAESTRE (O.O. 2nd Army Troops) for issue to 111 Bde. Scale of winter clothing for every Winter published in 9ROs – accompaniment accompany.	cont.

Army Form C. 2118.

WAR DIARY
or
INTELLIGENCE SUMMARY.
(Erase heading not required.)

Instructions regarding War Diaries and Intelligence Summaries are contained in F. S. Regs., Part II. and the Staff Manual respectively. Title pages will be prepared in manuscript.

Place	Date	Hour	Summary of Events and Information	Remarks and references to Appendices
ST. JANS CAPPEL	18th	cont.	Railhead for Ordnance only (OUDERDOM) will be used from tomorrow. Intimation with S.C.R.A. re — demanding Gun Parts from in any active operations. Divisional Ad. Quarters.	MRS
"	19th		Q.F.18ph Gun completi for 13/123 Bde received. Railhead for Ordnance from today advance OUDERDOM.	MRS
"	20th		Usual Routine work. Divisional Head Quarters.	MRS
"	21st		Usual routine work.	MRS
"	22nd		18th Convoy for 13/123 Bde received. — also Wagon 7's for D.A.C. To MERVILLE for head fondane. 112th hy Bde moved into the line to the North. — incidentally ammunition lorry made to issue stores by lorry. Divisional Head Quarters.	MRS
"	23rd		Usual routine work.	MRS
"	24th		Usual routine work. Detailed 2 Ammunition S.S/ts — each of 63rd + 111th hy/Bdes to carry out overhaul of Vickers and Lewis guns while at Hazebrouck — cont.	MRS

Army Form C. 2118.

WAR DIARY
or
INTELLIGENCE SUMMARY.
(Erase heading not required.)

Place	Date	Hour	Summary of Events and Information	Remarks and references to Appendices
ST JANS-CAPPEL	24th		out of the line.	—
"	25th		1 Kitch Travelli Cooly received for 8th Lincoln Regt — nothing else of movement importance.	—
"	26th		Demanded and collected a Vickers gun (without spares) from 2nd Army. M.S. Stone to replace one of 112th Inf Bde destroyed by shell fire. Nothing else of movement importance.	—
"	27th		Preparation for move northwards — H.Q. will be at ZEVENCOTE — arrange location of advance Dump. DADOS 39th Div. called to arrange taking over on this movement. Decided to take over Advance Dump at DEZON Camp from 33rd Division immediately.	—
DEZON CAMP	28th		Took over from DADOS 33rd Div. — Drew and issued 10 M IX Cvfs, 2 18/n guns for 13 + C Battures 123rd Bde. —	—
"	29		Railhead change to HAEGEDOORNE. and arranged an arrangement of name from stores shops + personnel. BRULOOZE, Demanded by Wire, 2 Lewis 15mm arm our guns and 1 Vickers.	—

A5834 Wt. W4973/M687 750,000 8/16 D. D. & L. Ltd. Forms/C.2118/13.

Army Form C. 2118.

WAR DIARY
or
INTELLIGENCE SUMMARY.
(Erase heading not required.)

Instructions regarding War Diaries and Intelligence Summaries are contained in F. S. Regs., Part II. and the Staff Manual respectively. Title pages will be prepared in manuscript.

Place	Date	Hour	Summary of Events and Information	Remarks and references to Appendices
DE ZON CAMP	29		Coults to rifle and crrnd(?) fire - drew + issued from M.G. Store M.I. Some of our rifles were annealed.	—
"	30		Drew and 3" Stokes Mortars from Base to replace unsuitable (?). Gathered 4 Vickers guns from 112 + 115 Coys + carried out minor adjustments. Visited new Salvage Dump + made arrangements to collect stores available for issue in satisfaction of indents. Established " Unserviceable dump" in process of stores notified all in command of Coy on.	—

Johnnythenough (?)
Capt DADOS
37 Bat.
30-9-17

37th Division.

War Diary for Month ending 31st October, 1917.

37th Division,
3/11/1917

John H Howarth
Capt.
D.A.D.V.S.

WAR DIARY
or
INTELLIGENCE SUMMARY.
(Erase heading not required.)

Army Form C. 2118.

Place	Date	Hour	Summary of Events and Information	Remarks and references to Appendices
DEZON CAMP	Oct 1		Usual Routine work.	nil
"	2nd		Usual Routine work	nil
"	3rd		Collected kit bags from Corps Troops and issued to units attached for Instructional operations. Issuing artillery signalling flags and Watson fans to Infantry Brigades. A.D.O.S called and inspected Office Store and Shops — Corps Salvage Officer called also. Interview with A.A. + Q.M.G.	nil
"	4th		Vickers Gun (6.5 M.G. (a)) destroyed by shell fire — replaced. Several A/S Machine gun stores issued notifying receipt of same. Machine gun notifying cannots. Issued new barrels to Lnt M.G. Coy to replace those rendered unserviceable by barrage work. Nothing else of unusual importance.	nil
"	5th		Vickers Gun numbered to 247 M.G. Coy lorry came up and by shell fire. Sent to firm to cut mole for filling it with requirements of warm clothing.	nil
"	6th		2 Vickers Guns issued to 247 M.G. Coy to replace lost destroyed by shell fire. Made special issue of socks (from Divisional Reserve) to units in the line. Unusual machine	nil

Army Form C. 2118.

WAR DIARY
or
INTELLIGENCE SUMMARY.
(Erase heading not required.)

Place	Date	Hour	Summary of Events and Information	Remarks and references to Appendices
DE ZON CAMP	6		routine work.	my
	7		Collected 300 pairs Gum Boots Thigh + issued to Battalion in the line. — Issued Cartridge to reinforcements — Unusual Routine work.	my
	8		Returned and reissued 4 Vickers guns to the Brigade in the line. Nothing else of general importance.	my
	9		Collected 1000 pairs Gum Boots Thigh from G.O. X Corps Stores + issued them to 63rd RNDiv. Despatched 4 lorries & NCO to CALAIS to collect 1500 pairs of Gum Boots Thigh. Ammunition collected from M.G. Store of Lewis guns to replace 9 lost in action by 13 R. Fus. in the attack at the 7 instant.	my
	10		Visited 63rd Bn HQ & issued new issue of Gum Boots Thigh. Called you from of Gum Boots Thigh from O.C. CALAIS by lorry. Inspected Corps Salvage Dump.	my
	11		Annual issue of 15,000 rnds to all units en route to Slough. — First this of winter clothing scale. Divisional Head Quarters — Carnations — Daviness moves to cont —	

WAR DIARY
or
INTELLIGENCE SUMMARY.
(Erase heading not required.)

Army Form C. 2118.

Place	Date	Hour	Summary of Events and Information	Remarks and references to Appendices
DE ZON CAMP	11th	contd.	ST JANS CAPPEL area on the 15th instant.	my
"	12th		Visited DADOS 39th Div at ST JANS CAPPEL and arranged taking over. Arranged to Dump 30,000 Wmli Pants at ST JANS CAPPEL for issue on arrival of Division. Indentures of DivL Ballie Officer is am. 5- for dump of Gum Boots received from the line.	my
"	13th		Move to ~~DE ZON~~ ST JANS CAPPEL postponed 24 hours. — Usual routine work.	
"	14th		Moved rearers to ST JANS CAPPEL. — Vickers Gun issued to 63rd M.G. Coy to replace one destroyed by shell fire. — General issue of to the Base for 1 limbered GS Wagon (complete turnout) and 1 GS Wagon, both to replace ones destroyed by shell fire.	me
ST JANS CAPPEL	15th		Moved whole outfit to ST JANS CAPPEL. 2 Battalions left 112th InfBde for work N.E. of YPRES — arranged to issue Ordnance stores at KRUISTRAAT crossroads (S.W. of YPRES).	my

Army Form C. 2118.

WAR DIARY
or
INTELLIGENCE SUMMARY.
(Erase heading not required.)

Place	Date	Hour	Summary of Events and Information	Remarks and references to Appendices
ST JANS CAPPEL	16th		Usual routine work	
"	17th		Usual routine work	
"	18th		Collected a Vickers Gun from Second Army M.G. Store to replace a casualty. ADOS IX Corps visited officers, stores and shops. Arrange with 1st Machine Gun Middlesex Regt to carry on for me whilst on leave.	
"	19th		Took over duties of D.A.D.O.S. whilst Capt. Howes on leave. Secured 3600 horse rugs from Stores Three Armoured Cars sent to report to each Infantry Brigade for the purpose of exchanging all arms.	
"	20th		Received 15,000 blankets from Stores. Made arrangements for temporary storage. Issue issued to 111 & 112 Infantry Brigade and Divisional Units. Handed machine works issued Boro Mandato to 63rd Infantry Bde	
"	21st		Usual routine work	

WAR DIARY
or
INTELLIGENCE SUMMARY.
(Erase heading not required.)

Army Form C. 2118.

Place	Date	Hour	Summary of Events and Information	Remarks and references to Appendices
ST JANS CAPPEL	22nd		Interview with D.M.G.O. re bifords. Usual routine work	Offrs
"	23rd		Usual routine work. 30 S.A.A. boxes received	Offrs
"	24th		Whitten Clipton machines issued to 2nd Notts & Derby. Lester futures issued to 1/1 Side. Usual routine work	Offrs
"	25th		Lewis futures issued to 6/3 N.S. Rifles. 9 Lewis LG's for 3 B'ns from reserve. Nothing else of unusual importance	Offrs
"	26th		Summons S. Singh sent to No. 46 Workshop to instruct H.Q. on L.G. fires leads. Usual routine work	Offrs
"	27th		2 L.G's both with B.M. demanded for C 123 Late R.F.4. Cordite side bag. M.G. bags & T.M.B's complete with respirants from Divn Boot Repairs reported	Offrs
"	28th		to L.O.O. Usual routine work	Offrs

Army Form C. 2118.

WAR DIARY
or
INTELLIGENCE SUMMARY.
(Erase heading not required.)

Instructions regarding War Diaries and Intelligence Summaries are contained in F. S. Regs., Part II. and the Staff Manual respectively. Title pages will be prepared in manuscript.

Place	Date	Hour	Summary of Events and Information	Remarks and references to Appendices
ST JANS CAPPEL	29		40. Tread boards drawn from Stafford 720 issued to each of 62nd 111 Bde Schools. Nothing else of unusual importance.	Appx
"	30th		Returned from leave. – 150 men from 1st Manch. 400 Brazier received from Base for distribution. Divisional Hd. Qtrs.	Appx.
"	31st		Usual routine work.	nil

John H Townsend
Capt DADOS
37th Div.

31-10-17.

e. 2118.

War Diary for
November, 1917.

D.A.D.O.S.,
37th DIVISION.
No. 3/12
Date 12

John H Howorth
Capt.
D.A.D.O.S.

Army Form C. 2118.

WAR DIARY
or
INTELLIGENCE SUMMARY.
(Erase heading not required.)

Instructions regarding War Diaries and Intelligence Summaries are contained in F. S. Regs., Part II. and the Staff Manual respectively. Title pages will be prepared in manuscript.

Place	Date	Hour	Summary of Events and Information	Remarks and references to Appendices
ST. JANS CAPPEL	NOV. 1st	O.O.	Drew 110 Jerkin Packs from Second Army Troops at CAESTRE also 10000 fathoms of wire tracing 0.0. IX Corps/Gs for issue around. Instructions from "Q". Nothing else of material importance.	none
"	2nd		Received 18/m S.m. for A/27 Bde RA. Interviewed Staff Capt RA re Transfers of guns and equipment between various Divisional Artilleries and own. Divisional Head Quarters.	none
"	3rd		Visited A.D.O.S IX Corps - then to BAILLEUL for local purchase. Nothing else of material importance.	none
"	4th		Divisional Head Quarters - ascertained that the Division will take over from 19 Division shortly. No 8th instant. - Harrassed routine work.	none
"	5th		To HAZEBROUCK for local Purchase - nothing else of material importance.	none
"	6th		Learnt from D.H.Q that this Division will relieve the 19 on the 10th inst/July. Nothing else of material importance.	none

Army Form C. 2118.

WAR DIARY
or
INTELLIGENCE SUMMARY.
(Erase heading not required.)

Instructions regarding War Diaries and Intelligence Summaries are contained in F.S. Regs., Part II. and the Staff Manual respectively. Title pages will be prepared in manuscript.

Place	Date	Hour	Summary of Events and Information	Remarks and references to Appendices
ST. JAN'S CAPPEL	7th		To AAZEBROUCK to draw purchases. Usual routine work.	nil
"	8th		Visited DADOS 19 Division re arrangement transfer of Officers, Stores & Stuffs. Travel Demanded 18m 2pm + Carriages for 1132 Bde R.F.A. to replace one condemned by I.O.M.	nil
"	9th		Transport reserves + part of Staffs to LOCRE. Interviewed ADOS IX Corps	nil
LOCRE	10th		Moved Office & live stores to LOCRE. Usual Routine work. Railhead changed to RU LOUZE.	nil
LOCRE	11th		Moved Office to HdQts at SHERPENBERG - drop ammuny at LOCRE. Interview with DA QMG	nil
SHERPENBERG	12th		Interviewed ADOS IX Corps re departure of Sub Condr MASON. Just commissioned & Gunner Brooks + Gnr Russell. Drew Lewis + Vickers Anti Aircraft Sights from OPO IX Corps & nots bicomfelt bosale ammuny with "Q" for subst. Life is take over my duties on my departure for 14 days Ammunition Course.	nil
"	13th		Usual Routine work. Howitzers and carriages received cont.?	nil

Army Form C. 2118.

WAR DIARY
or
INTELLIGENCE SUMMARY.
(Erase heading not required.)

Instructions regarding War Diaries and Intelligence Summaries are contained in F. S. Regs., Part II. and the Staff Manual respectively. Title pages will be prepared in manuscript.

Place	Date	Hour	Summary of Events and Information	Remarks and references to Appendices
SCHERPENBERG	13th		ref. for D/123. RFA.	my
"	14th		Arrived with DIVL O.S 39th Div. to take over dump at DE ZON Camp on the 16th instant. Divisional QMs.	my
"	15th		Handed over to 1st Taylor Middlesex Regt. Left for Connex in Ammunits at No 14 Ordnance Dépôt.	Ref
"	16th		Arranging tram stores & keeping trams hours to DE ZON & supervising trams into dump &c. visits to depôts camps & DHP	Ref
"	17th		Completed removal to DE ZON; visit to Army workshops HAZEBROUCK exchanging 12 Garden hose couplings by hidden the charges; 58 Garden hose having no section in hidden in Army for at Side &c. MASON repairing A.D.S. when arranged ammunits &c.	Ref
"	18th		Inspection panier expects to Arrived Camp; Ingress to work ext; visit to stopping &c; Supply HYMB infants the Misty on chief clerk; visit to B.8 Adv MDS & their track visit to DE ZON & visit to B.1 A.T. Coy R.E. for machine & skilled artificers to build camp for trams in at DE ZON; Receipt of 1,600 sets SD clothing & pulled on dump works moves; storing same at DE ZON; run section to huts dumps on use of hot disinfector	Ref
"	19th		Preparing trans locate refresher sharp at DE ZON; visits to KEMMEL dumps & arranging to collect all U/S Q stores & trans from B2 & 112 travails as informed to inspect DE ZON 21st visit to trans & anti trans; let tram formed to take up his quarters in my cpt	Ref
"	20th		Visits to No 18 Mobile Light workshops near VIERSTRAAT; also to 9 N Staff; round stores & buckle kept; visit to Q;	Ref
"	21st		Demanding Disk light No 7 for D/123; visit to Salvage dump at LAITERIE also to light dump at HAEGEDOORNE & to O.O. Corps Depôt for HOTCHKISS feed; visit to 112 Adv KEMMEL.	Ref
"	22nd			

Instructions regarding War Diaries and Intelligence Summaries are contained in F. S. Regs., Part II. and the Staff Manual respectively. Title pages will be prepared in manuscript.

WAR DIARY
or
INTELLIGENCE SUMMARY.

(Erase heading not required.)

Army Form C. 2118.

Place	Date	Hour	Summary of Events and Information	Remarks and references to Appendices
SCHERPENBERG	23		Obtd Latrine buckets & gas blankets through ADOS : visit to HAZEBROUCK with Lt EGGLESTON 123 Bde RFA to RE workshops with reference to an invention : exchanging 4 empty Strombos horn cylinders for charged ones at Heavy Ordnance workshops : visit to Divl lining near BERTHEN ditto 2 L.Gs made up in Armourer's Shop.	[illegible]
	24		Engaged in Stores & workshops : heavy indent from 8 Ed hands for L.G. replacements £200 worth : consulting AA & QMG who arranged GOC Bde shd investigate & report : conference with Capt Akerman 63 Tm Battn on sling for firing Stokes gun & arranging to make leather pattern for trial : visit to DAC	[illegible]
	25		Reorganization B echelon DAC into SAA Sect working out reduction wagons saddlery harness : K.T body for 8 limbers & 8 [illegible] reels : after consultation with G passing indent for 18 Strombos horns : round DEZON camp with DADVS : visit DHQ.	[illegible]
	26		Engaged in Stores & workshops : visit with DADVS to Clipping Establishment & Mob. Vet. Sec : conference with ADOS on various outstanding points especially as to provision of material for white patrol suits : consulting DMGO as to glycerine for Vickers guns in frosty weather & he decided 30 galls a week wld be necessary.	[illegible]
	27		Visit to DHQ discussing outstanding matters : AA & QMG wanted each battn to have L.G. for anti-aircraft work made up from salved guns : visit to 112 Bde & lines in reserve area : to wagon lines 124 Bde : subsequently to 111 Bde HQ	[illegible]
	28		Visit to Salvage dump : drawing 1000 prs gum boots & deliy Kennel drying room : visit to M.G. Store & drawing L.G. complete for 11 Warwicks : rendering special return of outstanding indents for guns carriages etc : ascertaining winter requirements for marquees & store tents	[illegible]
	29		Engaged in Stores & workshops : visit to DHQ : also to Field Ambulances : superintending loading 1100 tents etc : on trucks at ELZENWALLE collected by 112 Bde from Divl area on giving up canvas camps : making arrangements for building at DE ZON store for reserve S.D. clothing.	[illegible]
	30		Visit to Salvage dump LAITERIE collecting 3 Soyer stoves Soldier rifles etc : taking tents dumped there by mistake to ELZENWALLE & arranging for surplus from y'day & additional ones to be trucked tomorrow : reporting result to ADOS : collecting Store tents & marquees : making final pattern L.G. sling : going into question F.S. boots with DAC.	[illegible]

John H. Howarth[illegible]
Capt DADOS
37 Div.

1-12-17

A5834 Wt. W4973/M687 750,000 8/16 D. D. & L. Ltd. Forms/C.2118/13.

D.A.G.
   3rd Echelon

4 | D.A.D.O.S., 37th DIVISION. No. 8 Date 8215

Herewith A.F.C. 2118
for month of December,
please.

31/12/191/

John Hopworth
D.A.D.O.S. 37 Div. Capt

WAR DIARY Army Form C. 2118.
or
INTELLIGENCE SUMMARY.
(Erase heading not required.)

DA/OE37D
JW 28

Place	Date	Hour	Summary of Events and Information	Remarks and references to Appendices
SHERPENBERG	Dec. 1st		Returned from No.14 Ordnance Depot and took over from Lt. Tozer who acted as DADOS during my absence.	nil
"	2nd		Usual Routine work.	nil
"	3rd		Thoroughly inspected shops; tailors with a view to improving conditions + tonality amongst workmen. Interview with D.A.D.O.S. on various subjects. Visited No.54 Ordnance Mobile Workshop; ascertained that Wksp were leaving the Corps.	nil
"	4th		Usual routine — compiled Imprest Account + forwarded to Staff Paymaster Ve Cleary Home Base.	nil
"	5th		Visited Salvage Dump at the LAITERIE — also the Divisional Boot Store at KENNEL CHATEAU. Collected furniture for Hutment from OO IX Corps Tps and issued to Troops.	nil
"	6th		Interview with Staff Captain R.A. — Demanded 3 18pr Guns + 1 18pr carriage to replace "Seven" "shell fire". Visited No.3 Coy Div Train to render cheerfulness. Arranged for collection + disposal of surplus kitbags in possession of N.Staffs and 13 War Fus.	none

WAR DIARY
or
INTELLIGENCE SUMMARY.

Army Form C. 2118.

Place	Date	Hour	Summary of Events and Information	Remarks and references to Appendices
SCHERPENBERG	7th	7h	Visited ADMS IX Corps — then O/o IX Corps T.S. — afterwards to HAZEBROUCK for Lorie hen'chiney. Usual routine work.	—
"	"	8h	18th gun demanded from B/123 on 1,501's condemnation	—
"	"	9h	Interview with StaffCapt 111 Bde — also o/c No 3 Coy Dub train	—
"	"	10h	3 15h guns and 1 carriage received from Base in satisfactory ablitional nature. Usual routine work. 19 pounded Artillery transferred to new forGuanance administration. Interview with A at 9.15	—
"	"	11h	Usual Routine work.	—
"	"	12h	Usual Routine work.	—
"	"	13h	Usual Routine work — was told A/123, D/124 Bdes RFA + No 1147 Coy DivTrain	—
"	"	14h	Transferred A/S.Cdn. Hynd to DADOS 58 Div in ambulance with maint'-nus. Nothing else of mineral importance.	—
"	"	15h	Capt MARVIN reported for attachment structure. Usual routine work, A/S.Cdn BUTLER reported for duty from HAVRE in place of A/S.Cdn HYND.	—
"	"	16h	Usual routine work.	—

Army Form C. 2118.

WAR DIARY
or
INTELLIGENCE SUMMARY.
(Erase heading not required.)

Instructions regarding War Diaries and Intelligence Summaries are contained in F. S. Regs., Part II. and the Staff Manual respectively. Title pages will be prepared in manuscript.

Place	Date	Hour	Summary of Events and Information	Remarks and references to Appendices
SCHERPENBERG	17th		Visited Salvage Officer and Salvage Dump at YORK HOUSE, Interview with Staff Capt R.E. Nothing else of unusual importance.	—
"	18th		Usual routine work.	—
"	19th		Issued 125 F.S. tents from G.O.IX Corps Troops for use in billets. Dis- covered system of 13th Div. privately owned shoulder straps & put with AA & QMG.	—
"	20th		Collected 25 Boches Stoves from ou IX Corps resvts. also 450 Brazzin from Railhead.	—
"	21st		Amongst distribution of Boche Stoves F.S. Lamps & Brazzins to troops. Interview with Corps Medical gun Officer, 9.50, and D.H.90 re AA sights and Mountings.	—
"	22nd		Inspected TOURNAI + PARRET camps with a view to deciding what style of camp furniture they required. Administrative Conference.	—
"	23rd		Visited 111th Bde. H.Q. also RIDGEWOOD CAMPS — re provision of more furniture. Usual Routine work.	—
"	24th		Returned 15 ADOS IV Corps on defects in L.G. Magazines. Usual routine work.	—
"	25th		Nothing of unusual importance. Special issue of 25 Snow Relief suits obtained from the Corps to be issued to the Brigades in the line by car.	—
"	26th		Usual routine work.	—

Army Form C. 2118.

WAR DIARY
or
INTELLIGENCE SUMMARY.
(Erase heading not required.)

Place	Date	Hour	Summary of Events and Information	Remarks and references to Appendices
SHERPENBERG	27		Moved 19th Div. Artillery to DADOS 19th Div. Nothing else of unusual importance.	—
"	28th		To CALAIS to obtain 250 Snow Suits urgently required to enable relief of men in "shell hole line" to take place — snows being thick. — Issued suits to the relieving Brigade.	—
"	29h		ADOS 1X Corps called to discuss various matters.	—
"	30th		Collected 125 Snow Suits from the line & reissued them to DADOS 30th Division.	—
"	31st		To BAILLEUL and HAZEBROUCK for local purchase. 4th Australian Artillery transferred to me for Ordnance administration. Will DADOS 4th Australian Division.	—

Johnny work
Capt DADOS
37 Div.
1—1—18.

WAR DIARY
or
INTELLIGENCE SUMMARY.
(Erase heading not required.)

Army Form C. 2118.

DADOS 37D 37
VOL 29

Place	Date	Hour	Summary of Events and Information	Remarks and references to Appendices
SHERPENBERG	1st January 1918		Usual routine work.	nil
"	2nd		Wounded Salvage Stores from new dump at VOORMEZEELE. Enquires of DADOS.O. & ADOS IX Corps Office re disposes of various guns taken & in particular Area Stories & Transfers of Artillery & infantry. Nothing of unusual importance.	nil
"	3rd			nil
"	4th		To BLARINGHEM to arrange with DADOS 28th Div the taking over of office stores & shops. Conference at ADOS IX Corps re Artillery changes.	nil
"	5th		Assistant Inspector of Armourers 4th Army called re inspection of Divl Armourers shops. Manual Routine work. 15/hrs to replace these condemned by DVAO Denselder 3	nil
"	6th		Usual routine work - arranging for the move to BLARINGHEM	nil
"	7th		Nothing of unusual importance.	nil
"	8th		Moved 37 Divl Artillery 15 DADOS 28 Divn. Sent advance party to BLARINGHEM in charge of Capt MARVIN AOD.	nil

Army Form C. 2118.

WAR DIARY
or
INTELLIGENCE SUMMARY.
(Erase heading not required.)

Instructions regarding War Diaries and Intelligence Summaries are contained in F.S. Regs., Part II. and the Staff Manual respectively. Title pages will be prepared in manuscript.

Place	Date	Hour	Summary of Events and Information	Remarks and references to Appendices
SHEKPENBERG	9h		Interview DADOS of Australian Division for instructions from one. 11" notified Base by wire. Arranged to hand over my present office, stores, etc to DADOS of Australian Divn on the 11" instant. Defaulting Box reaches reserve to BLARINGHEM and fixed up with Camp Commandant the accommodation at BLARINGHEM from the Gehmaer Detachmt. Railhead Commanders DICKEBUSH	ms
	10h		Many numbers of wounded - shops to BEZON. Nothing else of unusual importance. Railhead Commander	ms
BLARINGHEM	11h		BEBBINGHEM. 11 mm of R.F.A reported for course in Hotchkiss Gun. Moved office + remainder of detail to BLARINGHEM. Informed Army and Corps of new location. Handed over to Aust. Divn.	ms
	12h		Settling down - generally - remainder of DADS arrived.	ms
	13h		Nothing of unusual importance.	ms
	14h		Scheme for overhauling all Telescopic Rifles in Division - commenced with 112" Bde. Have continue work.	ms

Army Form C. 2118.

WAR DIARY
or
INTELLIGENCE SUMMARY.
(Erase heading not required.)

Instructions regarding War Diaries and Intelligence Summaries are contained in F. S. Regs., Part II. and the Staff Manual respectively. Title pages will be prepared in manuscript.

Place	Date	Hour	Summary of Events and Information	Remarks and references to Appendices
BLARINGHEM	15th		Arrangements for inspection & checking of all stores in possession of M.G. Coys. Tested the new (R=A) advancing course in Hotak/KISS area. Army HQ furniture for huts being erected in this area.	nauce
"	16th		To ST. OMER for Local purchase. Interview with AA + QMG re infections.	my
"	17th		Nothing of unusual importance.	nauce.
"	18th			nauce
"	19th		Inspected the Arms + Accoutrements of 63rd + 247th M.G. Coys. Inspected Harness & Saddlery of 63rd + 247th M.G. Coys. Ammunition for Trench Mortar Batteries. Visited No 1st O.M.W 16 which all which for retain and not with H. Division is in want.	
"	20th		Continued with inspection of equipment of 63rd + 247th M.G. Coys — (Ruguinding & Signalling stones). Visited 111th South HQ re infection.	my
"	21st		Completed inspection of 63rd + 247th M.G. Coys. Instructed OC 111th + 112th M.G. Coys. C/S MARVIN left for GODEWAERSVELDE re inspection of D.D.O.S. Fourth Army.	my
"	22nd		Inspection of 111th + 112th M.G. Coy. Visited OC 111th T.M.B5; also 112th T.M.B5 to arrange for inspection of their equipment. Nothing else of unusual importance.	my

WAR DIARY
or
INTELLIGENCE SUMMARY.
(Erase heading not required.)

Army Form C. 2118.

Place	Date	Hour	Summary of Events and Information	Remarks and references to Appendices
BLARINGHEM	23rd		Continued with inspection of equipment. Arranged for course in "Bar" and Hotchkiss at the Hotchkiss Sqn for selected men from Divisional Artillery. Visited ADOS IX Corps.	N
"	24th		Continued with inspection of 111 + 112 M.G. Coys. – Nothing else of unusual importance.	N
"	25th		Inspected equipment of 63rd, 111, & 112 MGCos. Interview with AAQMG.	N
"	26th		Made routine work.	N
"	27		Received further from MERVILLE for finishing new huts erected in the Area.	N
"	28th		Handing over to Capt Boyle. R.F. Bde who will act as DADOS during my absence on leave.	N
"	29		Kanal Runkin Rounds. Started filling Lewis Guns of 111th Lt Bde with new L.G. Catches. Went on to visit	(B)
"	30		2nd S Course in Cam. Instruction of Hotchkins Gun Finished. Continued with 111th LBty Lewis Gun Latches Filter. Collected with me from MERVILLE the new huts in the area.	(A)

Army Form C. 2118.

WAR DIARY
or
INTELLIGENCE SUMMARY.
(Erase heading not required.)

Place	Date	Hour	Summary of Events and Information	Remarks and references to Appendices
BERINGHEN	31st		Capt MARVIN reported back to 4th the Army Cleary Depôt. 111. Lt. Bryant Lewis Guns were ordered with Collected from 9th Corps Troops for trucks in this area.	(P)

Charles Royle Capt.
A/ADMS. 37th Div
31-1-18.

WAR DIARY.

for

FEBRUARY 1918

From :- D. A. D. O. S.,

37th DIVISION

WAR DIARY
or
INTELLIGENCE SUMMARY.
(Erase heading not required.)

Army Form C. 2118.

Place	Date	Hour	Summary of Events and Information	Remarks and references to Appendices
BLARINGHEM	1st Feb.		Captain Marwin went to DICKEBUSCH to take over the equipment of 1st & 8th East Lancs. This is the first Battn. to be split up into its new organisation. 9th Division wanted working parties finished 2 Sec. 9 11th ed. Bde. all new but weather being put on.	(A)
"	2nd "		Long rout up to collect the equipment which is being withdrawn to the 8th East Lanc. better class of mineral water. G.	(B)
"	3rd "		To ZEEVGOTEN & sea 112th Inf. Bde. 15 & 11th Batt. Royal Warwickshire Regt. with regard to the being bitten up, made necessary arrangements with Q.M. Runton work. 6 B.R reported to Div. Cmd. for Change in Workshire fun.	(B)
"	4th "		with drew equipment of 10th York & Lancs. Regt. all being checked by 8th East Lancs disbanded. Capts. Marwin & T.A.O. 2nd Course in Workshire fun the Division from 29th Division 1st Batt. Essex Regiment joined.	(C)
"	5th "		31 R.Gs. with magazine spare parts Gunflats were returned to Mrs. Gun park. Also indigo[?] equipment of the 11th Royal Warwicks was into Store. Store Common Tools Sept. reported in accordance with order LNo.5 Gun Park GODEWAERSVELDE gifted one Batt. 63rd Inf. Bdr. with new L.G. instructed.	(D)
"	6th "		Litter Second Batt. 63rd Inf. Bde. with new Lewis Gun belts etche. 10: York & Lancs. Batt. also Dr.S. loaded two batns. Interviewed Quartermasters of 12th Essex Regt. owing to equipment in transit work. to their having been in the line sometime and insist unanpelled, hearing alterations expected.	(D)

Army Form C. 2118.

WAR DIARY
or
INTELLIGENCE SUMMARY.
(Erase heading not required.)

Instructions regarding War Diaries and Intelligence Summaries are contained in F. S. Regs., Part II. and the Staff Manual respectively. Title pages will be prepared in manuscript.

Place	Date	Hour	Summary of Events and Information	Remarks and references to Appendices
BLARINGHEM	Feb 7th		8th Royal Warwickshire Regt. disbanded. Littered third Battn. 9/63rd Inf. Bde. with new butt. Catch for three Lewis Guns.	(B)
"	" 8th		Roads 3rd Battn. equip. went into the truck for Calais. Usual routine work. 16 Lewis Guns & 112 Royal War miles dispatched to the front at GODEWAERSVELDE	(B)
"	" 9th		1st Batt. of the 112th Inf. Bde. had new Butt outfit fitted & Lewis Guns. Notify front of importance items. Usual routine work.	(B)
"	" 9th		3rd Course of Irish with to Div. Arty. to hatches sun Tin is led. All L.G's Batt in Division in Complete with new Butt outfit. Usual routine work. 9th M. Staffs (Pioneers) to be Complete.	(B)
"	" 10th		Usual routine work.	(B)
"	" 11th		Went up to WEST OUTRE tree D.A.D.O.S. 20th Div. with reference to move.	(B)
"	" 12th		Mobilisation withdrawn from the 10th L.N. Lancer. Usual routine work.	(B)
"	" 13th		Dispatches mobilisation Stores of 10th L.N. Lancs to Base.	(B)
"	" 14th		Handed over L.G.G. of L.N. Lancer WD.A. Gun Park GODEWAERSVELDE Handed over to Capt. Hunts on his return from leave.	(B)

WAR DIARY
or
INTELLIGENCE SUMMARY.

Army Form C. 2118.

Place	Date	Hour	Summary of Events and Information	Remarks and references to Appendices
BURINGHEM	15th		Visited DADOS 25th Divn at WESTOUTRE and made arrangements for transfer of Office, Stores & shops. 37 Div Artillery moved back 15 m. for adjustment, by DADOS 28 Division.	may
"	16th		Moved Shops & reserves to WESTOUTRE, interchanging lorries with DADOS 28th into a lorry row my charge S.C.	ans
WESTOUTRE	17th		Moved stores and office to WESTOUTRE. - Settling down. Kneed for Cooks & Divisional Salvage Dump's is the omitted daily.	may
"	18th		Interviewed Quartermaster of 16th N Lancs (now disbanded) re collection of certain items. Stores received from the Base - Surplus rum kegs been removed.	
"	19th		In accordance with Divisional instructions handed over "Gas Officers Respirators" to Divl Gas Officer. Nothing else of unusual importance.	
"	20th		2" T.M. Equipment handed in by Divl Artillery (unused) by the order for withdrawal of 2" T.M's from Medium T.M. Batteries. ADOS called and inspected office, Stores & Shops. Handed Cadun or ABEELE on economy they. Lt Col & late S. Dudley. (OC CALAIS).	ms

Army Form C. 2118.

WAR DIARY
or
INTELLIGENCE SUMMARY.
(Erase heading not required.)

Instructions regarding War Diaries and Intelligence Summaries are contained in F. S. Regs., Part II. and the Staff Manual respectively. Title pages will be prepared in manuscript.

Place	Date	Hour	Summary of Events and Information	Remarks and references to Appendices
WESTOUTRE	21st		Arranged with Area Commandant HALLEBAST for the evacuation of Office Store staffs at DICKEBUSCH. Infolk of Salvage Dump. Sent 5 An. Sgts and 5 O.R. i/c of 112 Bde W.O. to take over occupation at DICKEBUSCH — Stores for 112 Inf Bde Gp. Bombs etc. from An S.S./5 sent to DICKEBUSCH. Demanded on wire on 18th guns for B/24 — endorsed by QMG.	nay
"	22nd		Sent stores from 111 Inf Bde Group, M.I Bde WO and his clerk to DICKEBUSH. Remaining Bdes and Div Troops will be transferred tomorrow together with staffs and office.	mary
"	23rd		Sent remainder of offices Dumps and Stocks to DICKEBUSH. Staff (down General) — HQ Divn is now moves to CHATEAU SEGARD 25th instant.	my
"	24th		Interviewed 15th M No 18 Light Workshops — also or 48th Field Ambulance. Nothing else of unusual importance.	my
"	25th		Usual routine work — emergency accommodation generally.	nil
"	26th		Interviewed QM 13th Bn Essex Regt. — arranged to give reclamen Economy in Godewa Stores authorized.	nil

A534 Wt.W49/3/M687 750,000 8/16 D. D. & L. Ltd. Forms/C.2118/13.

Army Form C. 2118.

WAR DIARY
or
INTELLIGENCE SUMMARY.
(Erase heading not required.)

Place	Date	Hour	Summary of Events and Information	Remarks and references to Appendices
DICKEBUSH	27/2/18		Usual routine work.	7 HQ.
"	28th		Conference at A.D.O.S. – arranged with A.A.T.Q.M.G. for Lt Bromage R.B. to act for me during my absence on special leave.	9HQ

John Howorth
Capt DADOS
37 Divs

29 1-3-18

26

WAR DIARY

For

MARCH, 1918.

From:-

D.A.D..S.
37th. DIVISION

Army Form C. 2118.

WAR DIARY
or
INTELLIGENCE SUMMARY.
(Erase heading not required.)

Instructions regarding War Diaries and Intelligence Summaries are contained in F. S. Regs., Part II. and the Staff Manual respectively. Title pages will be prepared in manuscript.

Place	Date	Hour	Summary of Events and Information	Remarks and references to Appendices
DICKE BUSCH	1.3.18	2 P.M.	Took over charge from Capt Howells preceeding on Special Leave. Routine work	
	2.3.18		Received 2 stereoscopes on airaught objects received A/T 6/60. Received Bombing (advance copy) Topog & collected 3 scale range finders for anti aircraft work. & two flat periscopes for balloon officer's room in camp. Go Demonstrated interview Battery Lieutenant officer's & about 11am. the	
	3.3.18		Made arrangements about washouts of shell with men Command. Routine work	
	4.3.18		I turned O.C. Reg't M.G. Batt. signals, entirely suitable for M.G.s.	
	5.3.18		Supposed meeting of new 5th & 6th. Discussed the alteration of navigation 5th & 6th. Routine work	
	6.3.18		Routine work	
	7.3.18		Visited North staffs & correcting with return of stores & engagements. New pattern loose mud sniper collected.	
	8.3.18		Volunteer groups met & staff on engangraton on return from 9th M. staff to base. Supply-polished of M.G. Bath. returned to base. Gave OO at class to M.G. Bath. on motor trench junction.	
	9.3.18		Strip from M.M. column & emerald for Middleson 2 starter for T.M.B	

Army Form C. 2118.

WAR DIARY
or
INTELLIGENCE SUMMARY.
(Erase heading not required.)

Instructions regarding War Diaries and Intelligence Summaries are contained in F. S. Regs., Part II. and the Staff Manual respectively. Title pages will be prepared in manuscript.

Place	Date	Hour	Summary of Events and Information	Remarks and references to Appendices
DICKEBUSCH	10.3.18		50 sets Pack Saddlery for Coys issued D.A.C. & Army 77. Tramwater. Notice out	
	11.3.18		2. Hotbox & strength of officers verified. D.S. & A.S.P. visited Hazebrouck. M.tle Heavy Vehicles & driver return gas up latu.	
	12.3.18		G.O.C. Division inspected. Notice and kindred Salvage Dump. Interview G.S.O.I. Enquiry re equipment.	
	13.3.18		Inspection of equipment of Somerset womens. Corps of Division My own.	
	14.3.18		Interview with A.D.O.S. at Coys. 11 Bos. Changed in of boilers at Heavy Mobile workshops. Capt Nowels returned from special leave.	
	15-3.18		Took over from Lt Bromage. Nowne. nothing unusual.	
	16-3-18		Interview with A.D. & Q.M.G. - nothing else of unusual importance.	
	17-3-18		A.D.O.S. XXII Corps called & inspected office, stores & shops. Worth disturbed by enemy shelling.	
	18-3-18		Interview with Q.M. of newly formed M.G. Bat. 150th Q.M.G. and D.A.A.G. Hostile shelling continued.	
	19-3-18		Nothing of unusual importance. Hostile shelling again distributed wounds through the morning, aroused g. a.m. 8. W.	

Army Form C. 2118.

WAR DIARY
or
INTELLIGENCE SUMMARY.
(Erase heading not required.)

Instructions regarding War Diaries and Intelligence Summaries are contained in F. S. Regs., Part II. and the Staff Manual respectively. Title pages will be prepared in manuscript.

Place	Date	Hour	Summary of Events and Information	Remarks and references to Appendices
DICKEBUSCH	20/3/18		Wounds unfordable for all till 11 AM owing to enemy shelling. Reported same to AA&QMG & Asst DAG. Minnies & WESTOUTRE. Shelling renewed at 5.10p.m. Town direct hit – no casualties – some damage to buildings. Received instructions to move Westoute. Now comes out through damage to Material or Personnel.	✓ ✓ ✓
WEST OUTRE	21/3/18		attended conference at DAG office.	✓
"	22/3/18		Nothing at normal importance.	✓
"	23/3/18		Interview with AA&QMG – also D.A.A.G.	✓
"	24/3/18		Arranged to send lorries on "Economy in Gasoline stunt" to take place on 29th + 30th instant.	✓
"	25/3/18		Summarized into reports on scale suitable(?) for weekly issue. Visited ADOS and Corps HQ.	✓
"	26/3/18		Hard outside work. Suspended issues from Boots + Gum Rubr. Visited DATS informed by AA&QMG that Div will move on South at short notice – entraining 28th – Army's moving Second Blankets + tenth pattern notified to Railhead by all units. Transport refreshment, statement forwarded for to Asst Director Supr. battling to DADOS Tp Divs.	✓
"	27/3/18			✓
"	28/3/18			✓

Army Form C. 2118.

WAR DIARY
or
INTELLIGENCE SUMMARY.
(Erase heading not required.)

Instructions regarding War Diaries and Intelligence Summaries are contained in F. S. Regs., Part II. and the Staff Manual respectively. Title pages will be prepared in manuscript.

Place	Date	Hour	Summary of Events and Information	Remarks and references to Appendices
WESTOUTRE	28th	cont-	all kit, 4 stores + shafts cut down to lowest light. Arrangement for 4 lorries returned to us from MT dep. are attached personnel despatched to entraining station. Lorries loaded for journey in the morning.	—
WESTOUTRE - FLESSELLES	29/7		Found the MT Column at 7.30 am + proceeded 1st road to FLESSELLES - Third Army Area. Refuelled 15 V Corps at TALMAS and DAQ at DOULLENS - also 1st DAQ at TOUTENCOURT. Learnt that Guns in move to PAS tomorrow (IV Corps, Third Army). Received instructions in issue & transfer from Colonel Bonham-Carter. Detached Column and Lorries from Column + joined DHQ at PAS. Arrangements for refilling mts with Guns were taken in the morning. Reached WARLINCOURT.	—
FLESSELLES - PAS	30/7		Div. moves to SOUASTRE on HÉNU on the morrow. Refilled units at suffy refill points. Established Ammunition Shop at PAS. Arranged to obtain from there supplies loaded on at BRUHOOZE Railhead in Second Army before leaving.	—
PAS	31st			—
PAS	1st		Visited ADOS IV Corps. Instructions it mit, or orderly during state of Mobile Warfare. Arrangements for office to duty.	—

SECRET

WAR-DIARY.

FOR

APRIL 1918

From:- D.A.D.O.S.,
37th. DIVISION.

Army Form C. 2118.

WAR DIARY
or
INTELLIGENCE SUMMARY.
(Erase heading not required.)

Instructions regarding War Diaries and Intelligence Summaries are contained in F.S. Regs., Part II. and the Staff Manual respectively. Title pages will be prepared in manuscript.

Place	Date	Hour	Summary of Events and Information	Remarks and references to Appendices
PAS	1st		Visited A+Q's IV Corps. Interviewed method of handling when the movements in a state of flexure. Warfare. Arranged for offices & Buffs at COVIN, whilst convoy BMQ moved to COVIN on the 3rd.	—
PAS COVIN	2nd		Established Ammunition Shot into ammunition COVIN. Refuelled known stores & Dumps. COVIN — moved to COVIN in the afternoon. 4.7"Dis Artillery attached to me from Berles. 4.7" how. Collected 100 Trench Shells from one IV Corps Troops.	—
COVIN	3rd		HQ Divn established at COVIN. Interviews, BGRMS, AA+QMG. Arrangements for convoy of ammunition.	—
"	4th		Drew arms of H.T. Bells from GO IV Corps Tps. Visited 3rd Army Gun Park. Obtained Cups for firing rifle grenades had from them at DOVLIENS. Arrangements for issue of sorts to men in trenches — available interview Staff officer 111th Inf Bde.	—
"	5th		Established & issued 2 Vickers guns complete to replace those destroyed by shell fire.	—
"	6th		To 3rd Army Gun Park to obtain Stand for 3" T.M. Int. consignment from HAVRE & ROUEN received at Railhead. Nothing else of moment importance.	—
"	7th		Arrangements for collection of stations dumped in Second Army	—

A 5834 Wt. W4973/M687 750,000 8/16 D. D. & L. Ltd. Forms/C.2118/13.

WAR DIARY
or
INTELLIGENCE SUMMARY.
(Erase heading not required.)

Army Form C. 2118.

Place	Date	Hour	Summary of Events and Information	Remarks and references to Appendices
COUIN	7th cont.		Area.	—
"	8th		8 heavy guns demanded for east of 8th metres 88.1. Aeroplane took photos. 2 4.5" Howitzer compelled destroyed by shell fire, also one Howitzer only destroyed - demand to replace. Visited 3rd Army Gun Park at CANDAS	—
"	9th		2 18/hr complete of C/154 ordnance handed demanded. To GO. Third Army Troops PREVENT transfer of 37 Divl Artillery. Interviewed Staff Capt 37 Div Arty re deficiencies in armament in Thurnay Area.	—
"	10th		Arranged issue of routes to 4th Army with S.C. 4th Div Arty.	√
"	11th		Attended "Q" conference on arrangements for mobile warfare. Visited Third Army Gun Park re authorised material.	—
"	12th		Were at various work.	—
"	13th		18pr shrapnel demanded for A/123 Aeroplane observing shell fire. To DOULLENS for issue of howitzers, Arrangements for Howitzer to DADOS 42 Divs.	—
"	14th		Issued 1000 rounds of Gun Spl from O.O. IV Corps Tps. Made	—

WAR DIARY
or
INTELLIGENCE SUMMARY.

Army Form C. 2118.

Place	Date	Hour	Summary of Events and Information	Remarks and references to Appendices
COUIN	14th	cont'd	[illegible handwritten entry regarding Victoria Bgde., WTMS Bn., scale, ammunition, etc.]	
	15th		Final arrangements for transfer to COUIN PAS. [illegible]	
AUTHIE	16th		AA + QMG, also DADOS + 2nd DS + DADOS + [illegible] Transfers of offrs, staffs + dumps to AUTHIE — further movement of accommodation.	
	17th		Ammunition from [illegible] and question of accommodation at [illegible] Bns at 63rd Inf Bde.	
	18th		Discussed with BM, arrangements for 6/123 Bde FA'S — replace our [illegible] of 10th Rd — 2 Bns Am — LG's for C/124, [illegible] with Staff Capt 63 Inf Bde re Quartermasters of Somme Bns. Visited 3rd Army QuiRack [illegible] Som Bns on several Ordnance matters.	
	19th		Collected stores, any expected, reported. Prepared of Art. Aircraft agreement returns for Q.	
	20th		Visited HQ 111 Bde, also OC 15 R.B's and OC 18 R Fus. re Clothing, also our regm'l through to light sg recent operations. Interview AA+QMG re Rifles gas in Bucquoy. Nothing of moment.	
	21st		[illegible] Victoria Gun for OC 7 MGS Bn. Interviews with OC 1st Guards & OC QW Staff on general Ordnance questions.	
	22nd			
	23rd		Went through all Artillery entirely matters with Staff Capt HRA.	

Army Form C. 2118.

WAR DIARY
or
INTELLIGENCE SUMMARY.
(Erase heading not required.)

Instructions regarding War Diaries and Intelligence Summaries are contained in F. S. Regs., Part II. and the Staff Manual respectively. Title pages will be prepared in manuscript.

Place	Date	Hour	Summary of Events and Information	Remarks and references to Appendices
AUTHIE	23rd	cont.	Arrangements for new WPAS within the Gd gun in the left Corps Sector: Drew 36 Lewis Gun artillerie from No 3 Gun Park — to complete all Battalion to 24 LGs per Battn (including the 4 for AA work). Transferred Officers to PAS. Interim DADOS 62nd & 57 Divns.	✓
PAS	24th			✓
"	25th		Stores and ships transport to memo S. T PAS. Instructions to march from the matron of Special items of winter Clothing	✓
"	26th		D.D.O.S Third Army visited stores and shops.	✓
"	27th		Heavy aeroplane raid. Cee did 150 Gas Russes & 100 IV GTFs	✓
"	28th		ADOS II Corps called. Arranged cancellation of indents for handkgs & issuance of some tweaked over to 2nd Durany ink "stuffed gum" trolley at mesred experiences.	✓
"	29th			✓
"	30th		V. Cd Divisional Reinforcement Wing with reference to Germans Great coats: Interview with 10th No 28 OH W STRUTHIEULE re reproviolation re overcoats.	✓

Johnstones
Capt ADOS
3 Jans

1-5-18

DAG 3rd Echelon

War Diary of
D.A.D.O.S 37th Divn
for months of
May & June
1918

[signature] Lieut.

D. A. D. O. S. 37th DIV.

Indent for Ordn

INSTRUCTIONS FOR US

1.—To be used when indenting for Ord
**of Expeditionary Force:
Necessaries.**

2.—Separate indents should be prepared
Clothing and Necessaries, respectively

3.—Each indent will be made out in duplica
one copy being retained by the unit f

4.—Indents must bear a consecutive corps
identification purposes in the event of

5.—The necessity for indenting must be alw
(a), (b) or (c).

6.—Unless a representative of the unit atte
always be given of the address to wh
which required.

Forms
G. 994.
12.

WAR DIARY
or
INTELLIGENCE SUMMARY
(Erase heading not required.)

Army Form C. 2118.

DADOS 37 Div
May / June 1933 & 2/

Place	Date	Hour	Summary of Events and Information	Remarks and references to Appendices
PAS.	1st		Interview with DADOS 62nd and DADOS 42nd, Staff Capt 63rd Inf Bde, or 637th R.G. - also with O/c 37th Div about situation of issue of jerkins clothing surrendered by ADOS.	≈
"	2nd		Arrangement of transports connected by A/19 O about train journey from I.E.F. North about of personnel maintenance.	≈
"	3rd		Visited O/C IV Corps Troops, DOS IV Corps, Interview with SOS 37 Div about work at R.H.Q.	≈
"	4th		Manual munition work.	≈
"	5th		Interview both O.C. 37 Div Supply Column from at 10.57, No 258 L.M.O.V, took rate of mined maintenance.	≈
"	6th		Arranged from inclusion of N.C.O. of Div M.T. Coy in one teachers of Maddison's Gun.	≈
"	7th		Granted 12 6" TMs to re-equip X/41 + Y/41 TM Btys - shown 9" TMs having been returned to the Base,	≈
"	8th		6" TMs drawn from X+Y/41 TM Btys. Nothing done of usual maintenance.	≈
"	9th		To Railhead Chea to GusPards to discuss states myself myself cont.	≈

Army Form C. 2118.

WAR DIARY
or
INTELLIGENCE SUMMARY.
(Erase heading not required.)

Place	Date	Hour	Summary of Events and Information	Remarks and references to Appendices
PAS	9th		Nothing else of permanent importance.	✓
	10th		Nominal routine work.	✓
	11th		8 Lewis Gun sounded by wire telephone a similar number dropped by shell fire (13" RBs) during an attack on enemy post. Sasspwala opposite Pishin Bazar from Tirmandrelg.	✓
	12th		Visited ADOS 7 Corps also 0/0 IV Corps troops and O.C. 37 Y.T. Coy. Received February indents. Received orders to proceed to India at the end of the month.	✓
	13th		Most of 41st Div Arty. & DAOS 41st Div + returned all command.	✓
	14th		W.O. clerk skinman + toony (detached from Cadermore 41st Div gr) left Hy and for DADOS + Division. (Elected Arti Sin stores from O.C. iv Corps troops. Interview with GDOS IV Corps and AAAQMG.	✓
	15th		& the Division. Dined and the O/C Quartus movers to AUTHIS - annexure to be visit at PAS.	✓
	16		Usual routine work. Captain Morris proceeded on special leave.	A/6
	17		Received instructions at 32nd Division to proceed to Pas and take over from AADOS 37th Div.	

A5834 Wt.W4973/M687 750,000 8/16 D.D.&L.Ltd. Forms/C.2118/13.

WAR DIARY or INTELLIGENCE SUMMARY

Army Form C. 2118.

Place	Date	Hour	Summary of Events and Information	Remarks and references to Appendices
Pas	18/5/18		Visited Div Headquarters, A.D.S., IV Corps, and 111 Brigade Headquarters	A/6
"	19/5/18		Morning usual routine work. In the afternoon proceeded to Divisional Head quarters to take off equipment of 6th Bedfords and issue trestle equipment required for them including Div. Gas Officer, Engine Store	A/6
"	20/5/18		Visited Div. Headquarters, 6th R.B. Staff Capt R.O., O6 Composite Bn.	A/6
"	21/5/18		Visited Div Headquarters, A.D.S. (O6 Div train) & M.G. Bn	A/6
"	22/5/18		Morning usual routine work. In the afternoon visited Div Headquarters and attended two lectures given by Corps Chief gas Officer. Box Respirators were worn by all ranks in offices from 9.30 am till 10.30 am. S.R.O. 3489 dated 19/5/18 rather after. Div Gas Officer - B.3	A/6
"	23/5/18		Visited Div. Headquarters & the following units - 10 Royal Fusiliers, R.111 F de Headquarters & the following Cty - 50 Field Amb - 8 Somersets, 13 K.A.R. - 13 Rifle Bde, 111 S. Inf. Bde, 63 Div. Reg. + 111 Trench Mortar Bn. 8th Innis Drons - 9th Suld Accpt. & 37th Brig. Amm. All ranks to wear Box Respirator worn from 9.30 am till 10.30 am. S.R.O. 3489 dated 19/5/18	A/6

Army Form C. 2118.

WAR DIARY
or
INTELLIGENCE SUMMARY.
(Erase heading not required.)

Instructions regarding War Diaries and Intelligence Summaries are contained in F. S. Regs., Part II. and the Staff Manual respectively. Title pages will be prepared in manuscript.

Place	Date	Hour	Summary of Events and Information	Remarks and references to Appendices
Pao	24/5/18		Visited Div. Headquarters. Proceeded to 37 M.G. Bn. with A.D.M. Willett to inspect Vickers guns and Lecture men on the same. Found guns in a very insatisfactory condition which is due to severe general mud having to deal with them. 36 Lewis to severe general mud having to deal with them. Box Respirators found unserviceable. Box Respirators from tmy 9.30 pm Btty (103,67) (inc D 5/+89)	O/o
Pao	25/5/18		Visited Div. Headquarters. And II Corps (a) then proceeded to Workshops at Authuille. A a rgmy visited stores in the afternoon. Respirators worn from 9.30 am till 10.30 am (CHQ0&SP) General routine work.	O/o
Pao	26/5/18		Visited Div. Headquarters, A.D.V.S. IV Corps. Proceeded to Authuille (D.O. IV Corps Enrope) for A.A. mounting and new pattern expendable belt boxes for Vickers guns.	O/o
"	28/5/18		Usual routine work.	O/o
"	29/5/18		Visited Div. H.Q., 1st Debs, 1st Devt., 13th Royal Scotchers and 153 Bde R.F.A.	O/o
"	30/5/18		Proceeded to Boulogne with Captain Marsh R.E. & instructions for him to proceed to Marseilles for India.	O/o

WAR DIARY
or
INTELLIGENCE SUMMARY.

Army Form C. 2118.

Place	Date	Hour	Summary of Events and Information	Remarks and references to Appendices
Pas	3/5/18		No very usual routine work. Afternoon proceeded to Havard to arrange for despatch of Kaplets from Div Dump to Base.	A/6
"	1/6/18		Weekly Div: H.Q. Batto Officers and Salvage Sergeants meeting. D.6.29th Employment, Camp Commandant.	A/6
"	2/6/18		Usual routine work. (No car)	A/6
"	3/6/18		Usual routine work. (No car)	A/6
"	4/6/18		Visited Div. H.Q. Battn Officers. 63 Bde. B.O. Salvage Dump.	A/6
"	5/6/18		b. Rge. and D.R.O.O. Div. H.Q. moved to Lavillers.	A/6
Lavillers	6/6/18		Visited A.S.O.S. XXII Corps. Proceeded in D.6. Lynab Car. No car for remaining days.	A/6
"	7/6/18		Visited Railhead and N.O. for Mem Park.	A/6
"	8/6/18		Visited N.O. 63 Bde - 112 Bde, 111 Bde, and the following Sm. Draw - 153 Field Co: and 1st bourt.	A/6
"	9/6/18		Visited Railhead re truck of Clothing (Ling) and had cotton drawers sent to Battn at Authy. AWOL XXII called Everything found satisf. actioned	A/6
"	10/6/18		Div: H.Q. moved to Mieilly. Lus lorries sent out in des ordere from 6 (morning)	A/6

WAR DIARY or INTELLIGENCE SUMMARY

Army Form C. 2118.

Place	Date	Hour	Summary of Events and Information	Remarks and references to Appendices
Neuilly	10/6/18		Proceeded to Railhead 12 Noon & Stores from there received. Obtained 3 lorries from m.s. Bn. as one of W.A.O.S. was unserviceable, one at min POW, one sent to Railhead and one to Billeting Point. Finished clearing Railhead at 5pm - lorries made the way back with lorries sent to Railhead at 4 am to clear trucks (4 tons).	A/b
"	11/6/18		Two lorries sent to Railhead at 4 am to clear trucks (4 tons). Stores received on 11/6/18 and the 4 time drawn 27/5/18 were all dispatch to refilling points at 4 pm - a total of 16 tons. In the evening the lorry sent to duty with BRO. (No car) for lunch Rovers and one I sent for duty with BRO. (No car)	A/b
"	13/6/18		Visited new Railhead (Saleux) and Corps XXI Corps, visited XA, 111 Bde and 113 Bde and the following tanks, to Hd. G.S. T. Staffs, 10 & Bn at Fieffes, 111 & tanks, 112 & field ambles 110 LOO and A. elo.	A/b A/b
"	15/6/18		Usual routine work in the morning. Visited XA, 63 Bde & 63 D.A.C. (No car) Had to walk.	A/b

WAR DIARY or INTELLIGENCE SUMMARY

Army Form C. 2118.

(Erase heading not required.)

Instructions regarding War Diaries and Intelligence Summaries are contained in F.S. Regs., Part II. and the Staff Manual respectively. Title pages will be prepared in manuscript.

Place	Date	Hour	Summary of Events and Information	Remarks and references to Appendices
Nasiriyah	16/5/19		Proceeded to Basra Road at 6.30 am. Bus broke down at 9.15 am and had to make our way to boat H.Q. before being able to hire car. Arr. N.H.Q. taken in car with distress S.U. to return car which was unable to finish journey to Basra. Car was emptied at 5.15 p.m. and journey resumed. Arrived Basra at 6 p.m.	A/b
	17/5/19		Visited workshops and all stores carefully. One brought also workshops and all supplies when sent to Basra so as to be as mobile as possible. To see wounded Units to have more of the most them moved to Basra. More of the following Units: M.T. Corps, Sun Wing, Depot B.F.S – 13th R.S. and 13th M R.A. Boats.	A/b
	18/5/19		Usual & routine work. Visited 37th M.g. boys, mule arrangement to move late clothing and far stores to rear area. (No cars)	A/b
"	19/5/19		Visited M.I. Coy and moved all late clothing stores to Rao. Lorries did not return till 11 p.m. (No car)	A/b
"	20/5/19		Division moved to Rao area.	A/b
	21/5/19			A/b

Army Form C. 2118.

WAR DIARY
or
INTELLIGENCE SUMMARY.
(Erase heading not required.)

Instructions regarding War Diaries and Intelligence Summaries are contained in F. S. Regs., Part II. and the Staff Manual respectively. Title pages will be prepared in manuscript.

Place	Date	Hour	Summary of Events and Information	Remarks and references to Appendices
Poo	22/8/18		Usual routine work. No car allowed. In the evening a car was proceeding to Corps. Found that A.K.O.S. were on leave.	A/Q
"	23/8/18		Usual routine work. No car allowed. Visited Corps in the morning. 9th F. Staff.	A/Q
"	24/8/18		Usual routine work. No car allowed. Visited Corps in the morning. Saw the car taking the post to camp. Proceeded to Brigade H.Q. - Rashtrad and 29/45 Workshops also the following Units - R.O. D.V.D. - 1st Boer - 1st Res. 9th Full Ambulance - 37th M.E.M. Back spent it our small arrived new depot at Dept Park Government. Then proceeded to No 3 Dum Park.	A/Q
"	25/8/18		Usual routine work. Inspection of labour men this plain. 4 27th Div. H.Q. moved by the afternoon to Hemne in anticipation with Officers C.R.E. towards reports for Indies of A.O.D. on this source. Guns of Infantry over Indies of A.O.D. was told to proceeded to Div H.Q. with kept towards. Was told to see if anything was immediately proved to Corpo to see if anything was known about the meeting of Dept towards 80 for wanted.	A/Q

WAR DIARY
or
INTELLIGENCE SUMMARY.

(Erase heading not required.)

Army Form C. 2118.

Instructions regarding War Diaries and Intelligence Summaries are contained in F.S. Regs., Part II. and the Staff Manual respectively. Title pages will be prepared in manuscript.

Place	Date	Hour	Summary of Events and Information	Remarks and references to Appendices
Pos	25/8/18		On appointment as D.A.D.O.S. Twenty-four communication not allowed from 12 noon. No cars allowed.	A/6
"	26/8/18		Started routine work. Visited all M.T. as was left to proceed to 3rd Army H.Q. for my appointment. Telephone communication not allowed till 12 mid-night.	A/6
"	27/8/18		Proceeded to 3rd Army H.Q. as my appointment fixture to A.W. H.Q. turned. Applied for me to be posted as I had only five weeks to go before completing two years commn. arrived. Visited also M.T. Lapla Compan. 37 & Light Workshops and A.D.O.S. IV Corps.	A/6
"	28/8/18		Visited to D.I, 111th and 112th Brigade H.Q. as Railway Comm. and A.D.O. with details, also 29th Light Workshops to see "Reb" urgently as authd.	A/6
"	29/8/18		Visited No. H.Q. and the following Staff Captain &c. 37th Brds. Army Command cash, 123 Bdr. A.F.C. (Wagon Lines)	A/6
"	30/8/18		Usual routine work	A/6

WAR DIARY
of
DADOS 37th Div.
for
month of JULY
1918

Captain,
A.D.C.S., 37th Division.

WAR DIARY
or
INTELLIGENCE SUMMARY.

(Erase heading not required.)

Army Form C. 2118.

DADOS 37 Div
VK 35

Place	Date	Hour	Summary of Events and Information	Remarks and references to Appendices
	1/7/18		Visited No. 1 D. Field Bakery. Received and O.O. 4 & Ink Cards	A/b
"	2/7/18		Visited Div Hds. 103 Inf Bde – to dinner arhist kindred orders for Co E Inf (9) and to M.G Coy. On his return inspected the trains	A/b
"	3/7/18		Visited Nos MO – 63rd, 111th, 115th Frigade FO and the Infantry Staff. Captain RO, 9th Lincolns, 8th Dorsets, 10th Middlesex	A/6
			10th Punjab F, 13th Rifle Bde, 13th Royal F, 1st Bear, 1st Jarpa and O.b. Employment Coy to Trains at Bar Ships	A/6
	4/7/18		Usual routine work. Visited Q6 Rev Train	A/b
"	5/7/18		Called re certain stores. Visited 52 Workshops to make stars left by A.Dorsby for Captain R.O.— Q6 signal to Brigade Staff. Received, also visited Div Hds – M.g. Coy M.g. Corps re Experts and were Captain R.O. and 37th Brn. M.g. Corps. Also	A/b
	6/7/18		Aanaands for live stump chops	A/b
"	7/7/18		Visited Div. H.b. g, a, & I Staff, Baths officers, and 10th Royal F. Div. M.b. A.Dorsby, 37th Inf. G Q.O. brown Gum & Corp and 1st Bde R.F.A (Wagon Lines) and items demand of stores	A/b

WAR DIARY
or
INTELLIGENCE SUMMARY.
(Erase heading not required.)

Army Form C. 2118.

Instructions regarding War Diaries and Intelligence Summaries are contained in F. S. Regs., Part II. and the Staff Manual respectively. Title pages will be prepared in manuscript.

Place	Date	Hour	Summary of Events and Information	Remarks and references to Appendices
Pao	8/7/18		Visits Div. H.Q., O.A.R.S. IV Corps Light workshops & Kitchen. Travelled oft Lomnech and Reichen. Proceeded to Boulline to see way in try round for carry operations and collect information from several to station for some purpose.	A/6
"	9/7/18		(Arrived Div. H.Q. Vlog). Went to interview ADS at 6.30pm. Re. eye trouble, reclipation. Severe bombardier. Opposite to opponents. My difficulty with MS sore dressed.	A/6
"	10/7/18		Visited Div. H.Q. tour to met & stores required and MS and P Rifle R. is seen three tunes. Open park.	A/6
"	11/7/18		Visited Div. H.Q. Staff to Captain R.O. and MS up I. Full supply admis.	A/6
"	12/7/18		Visited Div. H.Q. A.R.P. and admis. At all OS formed. Afternoon usual routine work.	A/6
"	13/7/18		Visited Div. H.Q. Captain Edwards left for 74th Div. Ill. (Influenza). Lupino H.S. Wynn in Div. ordered to be	A/6
"	14/7/18		do	A/6

Army Form C. 2118.

WAR DIARY
or
INTELLIGENCE SUMMARY.
(Erase heading not required.)

Instructions regarding War Diaries and Intelligence Summaries are contained in F. S. Regs., Part II. and the Staff Manual respectively. Title pages will be prepared in manuscript.

Place	Date	Hour	Summary of Events and Information	Remarks and references to Appendices
Pas	15/7/18		Ill. (influenza)	a/b
"	16/7/18		Proceeded to A.A. 19 amy to Orville with the view of taking over a building as a new Laundry.	a/b
"	17/7/18		Admitted to Hospital (Pas)	a/b
"	18/7/18		In hospital. Nothing of importance to record	a/b
"	19/7/18		do	a/b
"	20/7/18		do	a/b
"	21/7/18		do. Able to visit Orvonne and to carry on for a short while. M.O. inspected camp. Found everything satisfactory	a/b
"	22/7/18		D.A. Army called to discuss various matters. Tried to hy work tub harvigero, but found it impossible. Obtained spares for tumbs to an old wash tub for Div. Laundry.	a/b
"	23/7/18		Visited Div. H.Q. Interview with M.O.G. & A.A. & amy re Lewis guns. Visited Staff Captain Artillery and A.B. 37 M.J.Co. – DADVO came to condemn 85 to apron shields unfit for re-issue	a/b

Army Form C. 2118.

WAR DIARY
or
INTELLIGENCE SUMMARY.
(Erase heading not required.)

Instructions regarding War Diaries and Intelligence Summaries are contained in F. S. Regs., Part II. and the Staff Manual respectively. Title pages will be prepared in manuscript.

Place	Date	Hour	Summary of Events and Information	Remarks and references to Appendices
Pns	24/9/18		Visited Div. H.Q. 111 Bde H.Q. O/C 10 K.R.R. - No 13 Rifle B. and Baths Officer (re opening of Div. Laundry).	A/Q.
"	25/9/18		Visited Div. H.Q. - Nos O/C 37th M.G.B. - 6.R.B. and Camp Cmndt. Had interview with D.A.G. re days for issue of issue guns. Smaller supplies G.S. wagons returned to Railhead.	A/Q.
"	26/9/18		Proceeded to our dump at Warnut with A.A. M.G. to check Ordnance stores himself to dump.	A/Q.
"	27/9/18		Visited Div H.Q. - Arm.s IV Corps, O.O. IV Corps, R.S.O. O/C H.L.I. his details, O/C 10th K.R.R.C. re issue guns and to discuss Bde cof's H.Q. 11", 12" and 43.	A/Q.
"	28/9/18		Proceeded to O.O. V Corps troops for inspt. Stores, visited O/C M.G. Corps re same, and also Div. Train.	A/Q.
"	29/9/18		Visited Div. H.Q. - O/C 37th Signals, Staff Captain R.A. and R.S.O. V. In the afternoon proceeded to Warnut to Div: dump to see what Ordnance stores should be returned to B.O.D.D. as owing to be moved.	A/Q.

Army Form C. 2118.

WAR DIARY
or
INTELLIGENCE SUMMARY.
(Erase heading not required.)

Place	Date	Hour	Summary of Events and Information	Remarks and references to Appendices
PCC	30/9/16		Received reintro bomb. Stores received from Div being coated with the rim of varnish serviceable. Ordnance stores to units. Breaches from which was sent in by OC "C" Coy sent in requesting that it should be condemned were tested with 450 rounds — no stoppage and 250 rounds were fired in the afternoon in the presence of OC of Coy. Gun is being issued as serviceable.	O/C
"	30/9/16		Visited By S.O. - Mr Kennedy and Capt E re issue of new S.O. Arms of foundry proceeded to Ordnance to [illegible]. Mr Cam knew of stores required. I bought to the notice of A.A. & Q.M.G. contrast & no special punch rec of stores required for Bren Guns. Bonn stores.	O/C

4

Diary of DADOS
37th Division for
month of August 1918.

D.A.D.O.S.
No. 51
31 AUG. 1918
37TH DIVISION.

WAR DIARY
INTELLIGENCE SUMMARY
(Erase heading not required.)

Army Form C. 2118.

DADOS 37 Div
Vol 36

Place	Date	Hour	Summary of Events and Information	Remarks and references to Appendices
Pas	1/8/16		Visited Sr. M.C. O.C. Div. Train, and O.R.P. and A.D. V.S.O.	A/o
Pas	2/8/16		Visited Div. N.C., Staff Captain R.A. sh. 37 Inf. Bn. Train Commandant, and Div. Laundry. Proceeded to Doullens to purchase uniform urgently required	A/o
Pas	3/8/16		Visited 63 Div. F.A. — 63 Bde. 111 Fd. Bn. 112 Bde and the following Units: 6th Amo. Park, 6th C.S.A present 6th H.Q. Squadron 7th & 9th Kent, 1st & 6th Buset, 10th & 13th R.Fus. and 13th Rifle Bde. and 63 Cos. 111 & 112 & 113 Batteries in the afternoon visited ADM.S 14 Corps, O.C. IV Corps Troops and Divl Workshops and sub Park Park Bn. 2. Lens.	A/o
Pas	4/8/16		Visited Div. HQ. & R.B. Light Workshops and Div. Rec. Camp. Dealt with some of the stores withdrawn from Div. during the general review recently. Remained on Camp all day to deal with the Units brought in to draw stores withdrawn fo.	A/o
Pas	5/8/16		Day spent from Rev. Saving	A/o
Pas	6/8/16		Visited AAQMG IV Corps Recruited light workshops Div. Reception Camp & Div. Laundry and the D.A.D.O. dealt interviews with	A/o

A.D. A...

WAR DIARY or INTELLIGENCE SUMMARY

Army Form C. 2118.

Place	Date	Hour	Summary of Events and Information	Remarks and references to Appendices
Pac	7/8/18		Visited Div. H.Q., Staff Captain R.O. & Gas Officer, A.P.M. the Baths etc. Since been out and 13th Rifle Bde.	A/6
"	8/8/18		Visited Div. H.Q. Staff Captain H.Q. 13 Rifle Bde. and [#] Btn. two A.R. Points. Also Town Major. Have visited new H.Q. and about to go down & see a and O and had interview with A.A. & Q.M.G. and arranged to move to new site tomorrow. Pgs. with reference re fifth division.	A/6
"	9/8/18		Proceeded to Doullens to purchase stores urgently required. Visited Railhead, 38/45 Light Workshops, and Div. Laundry. Had interview with Town Major Poc. with reference eight chairs at Herro for A.A.V.S.; also interviews with A.P.M. and Quartermaster 1st Essex re stoves =	A/6
"	10/8/18			A/6
"	11/8/18		Visited Div. H.Q., Had interview with A.A. & Q.M.G. and arranged with him to see Corps = the following In afternoon visited G.A.O.S. ≡ Corps	A/6

WAR DIARY
or
INTELLIGENCE SUMMARY.

Army Form C. 2118.

Place	Date	Hour	Summary of Events and Information	Remarks and references to Appendices
Pop.	17/8/18		In the morning attended Ammunition Conference held at HQAS at Achelus & in the afternoon visited ARPs and 8th artillery.	A/8.
"	18/8/18		Visited D.O. HQ. Saw Major Hems. 37th Inf. Bde, left H.Q. re outs ups of Ammunition to Bde H.Q. & to Bomaroto and 10th Royal Ir. H.Q. interview with A.A.Q.M.G. re duties of Ordnance in the field used the dep't until 8 became a bet. Re area visited Stores in the morning during my absence. Indian medical research were brought into a D. Half Light Artillery, which was had't into 2 Half Light Batteries) this matter had been brought to Le notes of Artillery turnouts.	A/8.
"	19/8/18		Visited A.D.S. & III Corps, right & light workshops in the afternoon. Also inspected No 4 A.A Inf. and ARS IV Corps. Also visited 6.30 Brukal AMP	O/8.

Army Form C. 2118.

WAR DIARY
or
INTELLIGENCE SUMMARY.
(Erase heading not required.)

Place	Date	Hour	Summary of Events and Information	Remarks and references to Appendices
Pas	15/8/18		Visited Div. H.Q. & 63rd & 111th Inf Brigades HQ and the following:- Staff Capt. R.O., 6 Rhys Bn, 13th M.G.K. B Cyclist Bn., 13th M.G. Bn. Arrangements to Midelous, 13 K.O.R.	A/6
Pas	16/8/18		Visited Arm HQ and front working party to arrange to carry out alterations required before ordering in the altered as attended conferences at Div HQ. First interview on packing case shows	A/6
Pleuve	17/8/18		Bn H.Q. moved to Henu - visited No. A.D.S. etc. etc. Proceeded to 29 III, 56 & no. 3 & 65 for experiment (urgently wanted - purchased) certain stores for use at Beaulieu	A/6
Pleuve	18/8/18		Reconnoitred in during morning - urgent business - In the afternoon attended Staff Captains Conference. Then proceeded to Rabat. 63 Div in administration of 63rd Artillery	A/6
Henu	19/8/18		Visited No 3 Gun Park to show stores urgently required, visited Obs. of 37 Major Lowton. Had great difficulty in finding them. 1616 gf dispatch form thanks to 17th what. (Which contains urgently required	A/6

WAR DIARY
or
INTELLIGENCE SUMMARY.
(Erase heading not required.)

Army Form C. 2118.

Place	Date	Hour	Summary of Events and Information	Remarks and references to Appendices
Nurlu	29/9/18		Remained in office all day to arrange things required. 750 waterbottles were drawn from old IV Corps things. Lorries despatched to Dutenne to collect waterbottles in 6's & 12's. Div think no 1st, 6 & 2nd Div. moved to VI Corps, so lorries had to proceed to Warlencourt Eaucourt for waterbottles, which arrived at 11.30 pm.	A/O A/B
Nurlu	30/9/18		Div. attached in the early morning and obtaining objectives. Arranged for extra Staff to be despatched to back, and also made necessary arrangements for a Rear Dump of stores not required urgently in case of an advance. Visited A.D.S. IV Corps in the afternoon.	A/B
Nurlu	1/10/18		Proceeded to Somencourt and district to try & get in touch with Units. Rear H.Q. to one of Army trains was urgently required. Visited 1st & 62nd, 10th Royal 4. and 112 Bde. H.A. In the afternoon proceeded to R.E. Station at Ytres amount to arrange collection at Warlencourt urgently required for advancing troops and then to Gun Park for 3 lorries of guns	A/B

Army Form C. 2118.

WAR DIARY
or
INTELLIGENCE SUMMARY.
(Erase heading not required.)

Instructions regarding War Diaries and Intelligence Summaries are contained in F. S. Regs., Part II. and the Staff Manual respectively. Title pages will be prepared in manuscript.

Place	Date	Hour	Summary of Events and Information	Remarks and references to Appendices
Henin	23/8/18		Visited OC. No 3 Coy train at Henin, and remained in the rest of the day to deal with stores urgently required for in advance, & arrange transport of ordnance stores as they were wanted for different duties during the day when it was possible to spare them.	A/O.
"	24/8/18		Visited OC train. Remained in stores for rest of the day to issue urgent stores to units. Great difficulty in finding transport as lorries were required everywhere absolutely.	A/O.
Longueville	25/8/18		Advanced Hrs. HB moved up from HB and DAD of to Longueville. Lorries from Magazines sent up at night to tank?	A/O.
"	26/8/18		Had interviews with DAQMG with reference stores required and General Ordnance matters. Moved two stores lorries to Longueville. (4 lorries).	A/O.
"	27/8/18		Two lorry loads of mundocks rugs moved from Bertha at Louraste to Advanced Hrs HQ Ordnance de Grand. Visited advanced HQ to discuss the matter of stores required by units, and arrange by and ordnance stores to the base. Visited 63rd, 111th and 112th Bde HQ and Staff Captain R.A.	A/O.

Army Form C. 2118.

WAR DIARY
or
INTELLIGENCE SUMMARY.
(Erase heading not required.)

Place	Date	Hour	Summary of Events and Information	Remarks and references to Appendices
Longueval Road	28/8/18		No cars available to proceed to per H.Q. 38rd IV Corps called and found everything satisfactory. Salvage dumps were visited and senior guns and machine guns and Lewis Guns were taken by artillery.	A/O
"	29/8/18		Visited div. H.Q. 63rd L.E. H.Q. and 49th Field Ambulance. Chose sites for stores when on march to move.	A/O
Achiet-le-Grand	30/8/18		Div. H.Q. 63 and Stores moved to Achiet-le-Grand. Visited railhead and arranged for truck for up the things for the Visited O.C. 13th Rifle Bde. 13th K.R.R.B. 10th Regt. & 63rd D.A.B.	A/O
"	31/8/18		and O.C. Div Train, also O.C. 37 & Brig. U.O. Trains bids Persian Salvage Dumps, had interview with Comdt. 9 & V. Staff in the evening.	A/O

Dados
37ᵉ D.I.
Vol. 6

Confidential

DAG. 3rd Ech. O/417

Herewith diary
for months of Sept &
Oct. 1918 — please

Bamford Comd
for
DADOS. 3/ Div.

31/10/18.

WAR DIARY
or
INTELLIGENCE SUMMARY.

Army Form C. 2118.

DADIS 37/1
Sept & Oct 158/37/38

Place.	Date	Hour	Summary of Events and Information	Remarks and references to Appendices
Brit NM France	1/9/18		Visited at Highluck etc & explns. RHQ. 1st Essex HQD.I. and 37th Bde.	A/6
do	2/9/18		Visited 111 Bde. H.Q., 1st Essex, 1st Herts and 112th M.G.	A/6
do	3/9/18		Visited 8th Lancers, 13th Royal F., 1st Essex, Staff Captain R.A. and Supt. Light Workshop. Advanced div HQ established and Supt. HQ. Passed warning to move and	A/6
do	4/9/18		Visited advanced div HQ.	A/6
do	5/9/18		Visited Advanced Div. HQ and Div't. bivt. RD etc No. 4 & 5 Areas. Moved 111 Bde. group by motor lorries & Gas store to forward.	A/6
do	6/9/18		Visited Div. HQ and Salvage Dumps. Fixed sighting pit at Taft. Mov. HQ forecast party to off at ernit. Left at camp.	A/6
do	7/9/18		111 Bde. Hm forecast party to off at camp to sleep. M.G. and chard out at sunrit to places in from Gh. mov. Knoll Spur above Gm forward and Hipho etc. Salvage Dumps to Devits salvage dump at Polush de Jouai to Round Down mining busy	A/6

Place	Date	Hour	Summary of Events and Information	Remarks and references to Appendices
Fovant	8/9/18		D.A.D.S. and store moved to Fovant. Visited 13th Bn & 1st Bn. On arr. IV Corps & district of scattered parties on two nights. B.S.H.O. to deal with same.	A/B
do	9/9/18		Visited Staff Captain R.B. and O.D. not H.Q. Long consultation with two ??? issues of extra clothing to various units. D.A.D.S. issued orders to all officers that all clothes formerly ??? must be renewed	A/B
do	10/9/18		Visited Divisional ??? ??? late 66 Div Area and 7th & 8th Bns Armdrly as ??? of ??? regards horses during the last three days at ??? Div Area and ??? Bos Officers. Proceeded to Yelw to inspect new site of camp to which ??? to move.	A/B
do	11/9/18		Visited A.S.H.Q. Dental ??? in hut officers mess hut and ??? store &c was at A.D.O. on ??? report also ??? and district. Div HQ moved to Yelw D.A.D.S. and stores moved to Yelw. Noted table & site of ??? towards to stores.	A/B
Yelw to A/Y/B then to A/Y/B	12/9/18 13/9/18		??? was ??? to approval no thing early sent to command to ??? for store in order and ??? mostly out to full accommodation. Camp was ??? during the night but road for horses. ??? ??? ??? ??? ??? man ??? ??? following afternoon. ??? settlement for one ??? no their ??? as ??? ??? ??? an afternoon ??? ??? ??? ??? ??? ??? ???.	A/B

WAR DIARY
or
INTELLIGENCE SUMMARY.

Army Form C. 2118.

Place	Date	Hour	Summary of Events and Information	Remarks and references to Appendices
Tetu	14/9/19		Point of view killed during the night so proceeded to Itivogue to choose and then at. D.A.M.S and also arrange to Itivogue with the Officers and evening Div. orders. N.A.M.S outcome of bath and 53rd Hosp. etc. In same the matter as sent down at not old stamp, as hard, this is last to this date, as small mess. Subject of the over of them. Visited 63 Fd Coe N.A. & 163 Subfl. R.O.	O/B
Kabayurof/Tetu			Visited Sir L.A - Staff bath R.A. - at HQ & sub Cinfls. 8th Lomondo and arrtd no buildings for store.	O/B
"	15/9/16 15.9/16		Visited Div. H.Q. - 1st Herts, Quartermaster's 13 K.R. & and arranged show do duty for troops at the A.v Batts. Village shelled & inhabits bombed badly during night of 15.9.16.	O/B
"	16/9/16		Visited Div. HQ - Div. Police Camp Commandant and saddler. Time at Rosheive Wood.	O/B
"	18/9/16		Visited Div. Batts. Will ride all during the morning for exercise. Went to Rens went at 9.30 am. Rest 3.15 pm. Visited A.H.M. IV Corps School near [illegible] [illegible] Arrivary [illegible]	O/B

A7092. Wt w478 9/M.2913 750,000 1/17 D&D & L., Ltd. Forms/C2118/44

Army Form C. 2118.

WAR DIARY
or
INTELLIGENCE SUMMARY.
(Erase heading not required.)

Instructions regarding War Diaries and Intelligence Summaries are contained in F. S. Regs., Part II. and the Staff Manual respectively. Title pages will be prepared in manuscript.

Place	Date	Hour	Summary of Events and Information	Remarks and references to Appendices
Ebensburg	13/9/17		Visited Div HQ. Staff Offr R.E. Ewarded to Co. 1st Inf Bgd. for night parties as Divisional in house with wash. Chief R.E. acting during absence	W.D.

DADOS:
37th Division

WAR DIARY
or
INTELLIGENCE SUMMARY.

Army Form C. 2118.

Place	Date	Hour	Summary of Events and Information	Remarks and references to Appendices
Vandelli	10/10/15		Coys. arrived at Vandelli on return from leave. Details moved from Ypres to Vandelli	A/6
Hancourt	11/10/15		Advanced moved to Hancourt. Great difficulty experienced with transport which unable to get stuff required from new dumps. Nett N.T.O's Staff supplied only from B.H.Q, and 39 Div. from same.	A/6
do			A.N.F.A. lorries were employed in carrying inadequate stuff from old dumps at Longueneuse to dump at Hapey and (?) that it was impossible to move the Advance Stores to Hancourt to Hancourt. All available men employed in above (as around Saint and running were in the Yard. (General instruction). One lorry despatched at night to Ypres half load. One to O.C. II Corps Troops for stores. Pates visited at Aigny and Lemotte and arranged about the at an undreds heavy booked R.H.Q. & IV Corps M.L. Feb. 13th R.B.	U.M.B.
do	12/10/15		13 H R.B. 10th R.B. and 10th R.B. and 10th Field Amble. Two Lorries arrived from Railway - Cd would "demolish" as no transport was available. Brought up at night to bring stores from Vandelli	A/6

Instructions regarding War Diaries and Intelligence Summaries are contained in F. S. Regs., Part II. and the Staff Manual respectively. Title pages will be prepared in manuscript.

WAR DIARY
or
INTELLIGENCE SUMMARY.
(Erase heading not required.)

Army Form C. 2118.

Place	Date	Hour	Summary of Events and Information	Remarks and references to Appendices
Haucourt	14/10/18		Visited Div Clipping Depot and store sent up to same, also visited Div Bath/Laundry and Laundry, Mobile Vet Section, 112th Bde H.Q. and 1st Herts. Supply Train did not arrive at the siding till 12.15 am 15th inst & lorries loaded back at 4. am	AfG
do	15/10/18		Visited Railhead and found things very congested. Supply train of 14th inst still in siding & train for 15th inst not arrived. About 20 lorrie loads of stores awaited from Base. The difficulty of transport & non arrival of trains brought to notice of Div & ADOS IV Corps, wired to Base to stop issues as instructed. Lorries returned from Railhead 8.am 16th inst	AfG.
do	16/10/18		Visited Div Baths, 112th Bde & 63rd Bde H.Q. 63rd LTMB(...), 152 Field Coy RE (...) 8th Lincolns, 8th Somersets, 4th Middlesex 13th R F and 1st Herts	AfG
do	17/10/18		Visited Div Baths, Div Clipping Depot 63rd Bde HQ, 103 Coy Train, 37th MG Corps, DG Div Train 1st Essex	AfG

A7092. Wt. W128 9/M1293 750,000. 1/17. D. D & L., Ltd. Forms/C2118/14.

Army Form C. 2118.

WAR DIARY
or
INTELLIGENCE SUMMARY.
(Erase heading not required.)

Instructions regarding War Diaries and Intelligence Summaries are contained in F. S. Regs., Part II. and the Staff Manual respectively. Title pages will be prepared in manuscript.

Place	Date	Hour	Summary of Events and Information	Remarks and references to Appendices
Hazebrouck	18/11/17		Visited A.D.O.S. IV Corps, D.A.D.O.S. Army Zealand about 4.5.2.2. Sets and various other points with regard to the alteration authorised this about of S.A.A. and spare limbs. He points it has forward recom was required Lt. Col. Kerr.	A/b
do	19/11/17		Visited Southd. D.A.Ds. 46, 59 & Divs., Div. Baths new Ranchy and A.D.M.S. IV Corps. Discussed Mr revolvers now acked to R.O.D.	A/b
do	20/11/17		Visited 63 D. Rdo M.B., 4 & 6 Field Amb. 49th & 65rd Divn 9,13th & 14th Fd Amb. Ancillaries hospital train 9 & Ru R.B	A/b
F.D.	21/11/17		Visited Div. Baths at Fegry & Bandry A.D.M.S. IV Corps 38+C. regt m/Mot Pl. 27, Rifle 4th Div. and D.D.D.T. re a suitable place for storee in re referred to Bandry to kind a suitable place for storee in case at a move. Visited 41st Field Aundry, 9th musters and	A/b
do	22/11/17		15 + Field Co R.B	A/b
Bandry	23/11/17		D.O.D.O.S. and Staff Major reported to Bandry, Visited new Bendhu B.A.D./D.D.V.S. Reports on inter views re Div Baths with A.D.S. 2nd Army and 37th Divi. Fel. Lend. Rauchy (Rauches) contpan pay both Received + visited new M.B. Ruashy + Rauches with K.H.B.M. as the Supply train will visit Fremby Rauchand at a time next five up. Wished tram to it. check Soundry at a time next five up. Wished tram to it. F. in directly N.H.C.B. Canarin train on home of m.t. when received,	A/b
do	24/11/17		F. in directly to Bandry	A/b

WAR DIARY
or
INTELLIGENCE SUMMARY.
(Erase heading not required.)

Army Form C. 2118.

Place	Date	Hour	Summary of Events and Information	Remarks and references to Appendices
Boundon	15/10/18		Proceeded to Brigades with the view of informing [illegible] to that have during the afternoon & found that the Welsh Brown Division hqrs had been handed over to the Div. Supply Column. Reported the matter to O.A. 14 Inf Div deemed not satisfactory and the difficulties in handing to lack of accommodation shown by [illegible] to Bebronnes was brought to A.A. & Q.M.G. noted.	A/O.
do	24/10/18		Visited Railhead, details Workshops and A.S.C. IV Corps re the difficulties with [illegible] but informed that actions were not [illegible] D.A.D.S. & T. Office work very trying – received outstanding Rations Etc.	A/O.
do	27/10/18		Visited Railhead re issue of ham clothing not arrived. Div. Laundry Landing A.N.L. IV Corps re difficulties with laundry – Arrived to proceed to Army & discuss the question. Visited D.A.D.S.&T. Army, 30 tents were drawn from IV Corps for accommodation for tea [illegible] at the service as M.C. was could be [illegible] at Reffilling Point so that Rations being sent to Units.	A/O.
do	28/10/18			A/O.

Army Form C. 2118/4.

WAR DIARY
or
INTELLIGENCE SUMMARY.

Army Form C. 2118.

Place	Date	Hour	Summary of Events and Information	Remarks and references to Appendices
Laundry	29/10/18		Visited Staff Capt R.O. Nos H.Q. Arranged accommodation for H.A. & O.S. at Prisches and stores sent down in the evening. H.A.D.O.S. and stores moved to Brooks. Visited Left Sect R.E. and Capts in absence of Major. To hurry clothing moved from Div. Laundry to Tronquoy on Reptiled Park Pres Truck.	A/O
Brooks	30/10/18		At Posts Division Hours Railhead Visited 87th Supple Coy, R.Pk, 70th Field Amble, & It will make Assisted Open Park No.3 (Cambrai)	A/O A/O
do	31/10/18			

DADOS
37th Division

O/665

War Diary.

November 1918.

D.A.D.O.S.

37th Division.

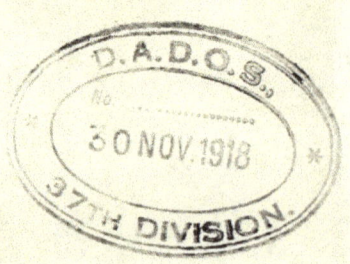

WAR DIARY or INTELLIGENCE SUMMARY

Army Form C. 2118.

Place	Date	Hour	Summary of Events and Information	Remarks and references to Appendices
Brads	1/11/18		Proceeded to Bruckney Stores very urgently required by Div. Returned at 7.30 pm	A/Q
do	2/11/18		Visits Corps IV Corps & OO IV Corps Stores re any entry required, also OMLs front Corps re following at night. Arrangements were made very hurriedly [illegible] to be encamped about [illegible] due [illegible] Corps troops. Hasty [illegible] inspection of stations re stores and [illegible] the attempt calculate on direct shelling from IV Corps troops. It was extremely difficult in time [illegible] to Supply [illegible] the mens and front of the orders (who directed) every[illegible] still find [illegible] inspection [illegible] [illegible] to area on [illegible]	A/Q
do			[illegible] to the divisional [illegible] branches which [illegible] did to arrange for a visit [illegible] it any [illegible] of the [illegible] from V [illegible] had arrived. Were collected and afterwards	A/Q
do	3/11/18		Nothing of note. Staff Clerical routine work and arranged for move to Tewville on 6th inst.	A/Q

WAR DIARY or INTELLIGENCE SUMMARY

Army Form C. 2118.

Place	Date	Hour	Summary of Events and Information	Remarks and references to Appendices
Neuville	6/11/18		D.C.M.O. and Staff moved to Neuville reaccommodating	A/O
do	7/11/18		Visited Corps Hqrs. 63rd & the R.O. 8th in room there. Routine work.	A/O
do	8/11/18		Proceeded to IV Corps to obtain from A.D.S. medal ribbons required for presentation on 9th inst. 1000 requires if no ammo obtained which it was impossible to obtain at such short notice.	A/O
do	9/11/18		Visited 8th Lincolns, 4th Middlesex, 111th to Field Hqrs and 13th Rifle Bde re ammo armour & ammo obtained N'Sons Guns, Parts & ammo Turno etc	A/O
do	10/11/18		Proceeded to Landry to arrange for stores & offices for Divns. Returned at 5-30	A/O
Landry	11/11/18		D.C.M.O. & Staff moved with Division to Landry	A/O
do	12/11/18		Visited Landry in truck & do things over & nearly had a numerous rest to dismantle huts etc & small injury from numerous trips. Programme went to (party) should be done by Programme. Things nearly finished taking from on 13 inst.	A/O

Army Form C. 2118.

WAR DIARY
or
INTELLIGENCE SUMMARY.
(Erase heading not required.)

Instructions regarding War Diaries and Intelligence Summaries are contained in F. S. Regs., Part II. and the Staff Manual respectively. Title pages will be prepared in manuscript.

Place	Date	Hour	Summary of Events and Information	Remarks and references to Appendices
Faudiny	13/11/18		The men indulged in getting everything ready for presentation parade to take place in the afternoon. Three Prisoners sent to fix Dispos on Baths at Rihencourt & three sent to dismantle Baths at Inseigner which from maps refused to hand over. The Army Corps of Tanks find clothing etc dispatched to base as they were to proceed to Germany as an early date. HQrs entrusive with various Officers & Tommies	A/6
do	14/11/18		Usual routine work. Made arrangements for the relief of Incident in a few days & demand on Base in view of moving to Germany.	A/6
do	15/11/18		Routine work very heavy.	A/6
do	16/11/18		Worked after smith two at Laton Indents very heavy or moving to Germany.	A/6
do	17/11/18		All – Refused to parade	A/6
do	18/11/18		do	A/6
do	19/11/18		do	A/6

Army Form C. 2118.

WAR DIARY
or
INTELLIGENCE SUMMARY.
(Erase heading not required.)

Place	Date	Hour	Summary of Events and Information	Remarks and references to Appendices
Infantry	24/11/18		March routine work. Men always on fresh work an Div is stationed in Banday, and every day have interviews with Division OC and Quartermasters Manual written work	O/C
do	25/11/18		do	O/C
do	26/11/18		do	O/C
do	27/11/18		Left in the morning in Ford to visit what a few outlaying in dumps that were waiting for Germans's surrender and were [illegible] an accident with an ordial Obsequ and was [illegible] buried an [illegible] in the arrangement was made at Albertville for transport lorry, left B.H.Q. with be lorry & [illegible] for Anceau on 27th to test as [illegible] Friday	O/C
	28/11/18		[illegible] [illegible] army [illegible] [illegible] [illegible]	
do	29/11/18		Back my from H.Q. Div Returned I.H. also found Ordnance [illegible] and Clothing Depôts to D.A.D.O.S. at Renaix (Ronay)	O/C

Army Form C. 2118.

WAR DIARY
or
INTELLIGENCE SUMMARY.
(Erase heading not required.)

Instructions regarding War Diaries and Intelligence Summaries are contained in F. S. Regs., Part II. and the Staff Manual respectively. Title pages will be prepared in manuscript.

Place	Date	Hour	Summary of Events and Information	Remarks and references to Appendices
Landry	24/11/18		Work & routine reports	A/B
do	29/11/18		do do Went to 87th Bn Hq. and on Rct	A/B
do	30/11/18		Usual routine work. Back hundred over to Lieut. Major Laury Richardson.	

Q.822./Adly. 40

37

WAR - DIARY.

FOR

DECEMBER 1918.

FROM:-

D.A.D.O.S.,
37th DIVISION.

WAR DIARY or INTELLIGENCE SUMMARY

Army Form C. 2118.

DADS 37

Place	Date	Hour	Summary of Events and Information	Remarks and references to Appendices
Boulogne	1/10/18		Usual routine work. 4 new loads of unserviceable linen and cotton stores of which had been authorized by H.Q.L.of C. were returned to the Base. 4 drivers sent on new course to new area.	A.f.b.
Yprenghe	2/10/18		B.O.B.O.E. & others moved from Boulogne to Yprenghe (E. Quarry) &	A.f.b.
do	3/10/18		Usual routine work. Kept Railhead (E. Quarry) & arrange for opening date at Yprenghe	A.f.b. A.f.b.
do	4/10/18		Usual routine work. Attended Divisional conference in afternoon.	A.f.b.
do	5/10/18		4 lorry detail from Moore cleared from Authro at night as requisite to R.S.D. owing to lack of accommodation. Visited 39th H.Q.L.of C. at Ypres.	A.f.b.
do	6/10/18		4 lorries dispatched to Laundry Boulogne to move clothing to avoid longer journey when new area is ready.	A.f.b.
do	7/10/18		Usual routine work. Loads sent to Laundry at Boulogne for items also etc.	A.f.b.

Army Form C. 2118.

WAR DIARY
or
INTELLIGENCE SUMMARY.
(Erase heading not required.)

Instructions regarding War Diaries and Intelligence Summaries are contained in F. S. Regs., Part II. and the Staff Manual respectively. Title pages will be prepared in manuscript.

Place	Date	Hour	Summary of Events and Information	Remarks and references to Appendices
Spermonde	8/7/18		Usual routine work. Two lorry loads of clean clothing sent to new area to be available for troops on arrival.	A/B
do	9/7/18		Wired battns for boots the urgently required. Usual routine work.	A/B
do	10/7/18		Proceeded to Moselle to find accommodation	A/B
do	11/7/18		Lorries dispatched to Laundry for clothing.	B/B
do	12/7/18		to Moselle with clothing. Arranged for to bring it up for issue. Two lorries sent to foundry for Laundry of Laundry. Two lorries sent to Moselle with Laundry. Laundry material was sent to Moselle for issue.	A/B
do	13/7/18		Usual routine work. Visited Hospital etc for stores urgently required by them, but could not obtain any.	A/B
do	14/7/18 16		Went through with O.C. R.A. P of L. Artillery Indents Artillery Sent to be proceed of stores. Ammunition sup.	A/B
do	15/7/18 6		to Moselle Moselle in absence our stores. Usual routine work. Will move to Lomme before	A/B

WAR DIARY
or
INTELLIGENCE SUMMARY.

(Erase heading not required.)

Army Form C. 2118.

Place	Date	Hour	Summary of Events and Information	Remarks and references to Appendices
Roubaix	18/12/18		D visited and gave away to Speeches	A/Q
do	19/12/18		Visited R.W.O. Charleroi and O.C III Corps troops	A/Q
do	15/12/18		Visited with baths & Laundry Officer the building taken over for Div. Laundry and Baths.	A/Q
do	19/12/18		to think of importance to report	A/Q
do	20/12/18		Div. gathers enough "kit" of South ... & knits of blankets & general stores. No. ... been returned from Base but do for none "yet" received. ... out lately.	A/Q
do	21/12/18		Actions HH. Gay & Nash & Further Major Rutherford. — No trucks arrived from Betens (... many) which No hand from Ordce Laundry assembled	A/Q
do	22/12/18		Field Rutherford. — 9 trucks received. — 6 kinds of blankets 1 Vehicle Derby & kinds about to be made were available from Ord. Arrange with R.O.D. to hold 4 trucks over	A/Q

Army Form C. 2118.

WAR DIARY
or
INTELLIGENCE SUMMARY.
(Erase heading not required.)

Instructions regarding War Diaries and Intelligence Summaries are contained in F. S. Regs., Part II. and the Staff Manual respectively. Title pages will be prepared in manuscript.

Place	Date	Hour	Summary of Events and Information	Remarks and references to Appendices
Boulogne	23/12/18		Visited A.D.S. M Corps and 28/45 Light Workshops	A/D
do	24/12/18		Visited Railway Sirks despatches from Rouen on the 19th and up to date. In-coming more frequent. 6 to 10 motorcycles to Signalman	A/D
do	25/12/18		Issued routine work. (Xmas day) mid-day	A/D
do	26/12/18		Four trucks of stores received from Rouen. R.O.D. shunters refused to take duty unless sent for to do so. Drew Lily St. Omer — trucks taken up with A.D.I.S. Moved routine work. Arranged with traffic for a truck to Laundry clothing to be despatched to No. Area Lady St Omer	A/D
do	27/12/18		Usual routine work	A/D
do	29/12/18		Usual routine work	A/D
do	30/12/18		Interview with Baths Officer re emclosed day visit	A/D
do	31/12/18		Routine work. Visited R.O. P.O. 111th Base H.O. & O.B.10 Ry Rt	A/D

War Diary

for

January 1919.

D. A. D. O. S.

37th Division.

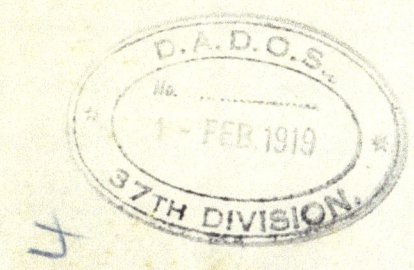

WAR DIARY
or
INTELLIGENCE SUMMARY.

(Erase heading not required.)

Army Form C. 2118.

WO 4 2

37

Place	Date	Hour	Summary of Events and Information	Remarks and references to Appendices
Hôtel Scribe	1/1/19		In chief office	A/G
do	2/1/19		do	A/G
do	3/1/19		Went through with A.D.O.S. Mg Cwolswicks Issues re clothing etc. Had interview with A.G. of 1st Batt re equipment	A/G
do	4/1/19		Three meeting worth. End interview with Quartermaster of Serbs & 14 Escar re civi & boots supplies etc. My could not obtain supplies from Paris & to investigate on medical with now statement autogranes and of report the matter to Kraaltd to staff boat to be placed in our frequently being made in the supt & being not to be reflect in front of the mats by letting this seem to be long	A/G
do	5/1/19		Heard routine work. Interview with A.D.O.S Duy. re Issued Indents of used Ordnance matter	A/G
do	6/1/19		Visited R.Q. 37th Div. Ord. #398 B.P.O. R.E. re opening depots to be opened	A/G
do	7/1/19		Visited 37th Div. E. Sonper - 11/3 Field Coy	A/G

WAR DIARY
or
INTELLIGENCE SUMMARY.
(Erase heading not required.)

Army Form C. 2118.

Place	Date	Hour	Summary of Events and Information	Remarks and references to Appendices
Epéhy	8/11/19		Usual routine work. Visited 37 & 39 M.G. Bn., 1st & 2nd S.G. Bn (re rifles) R.O.D.	A/6
do	9/11/19		Visited 9th M.G. Staffs. Attended conference at H.Q.	A/6
do	10/11/19		Usual routine work. Attended conference at H.Q.	A/6
do	11/11/19		Visited A.D.V.S. and O.B. Div. Reception Camp	A/6
do	12/11/19		Visited A.D.V.S. IV Corps and 20 IV Corps troops	A/6
do	13/11/19		Visited 9th M.G. Staffs re Officers transferring to R.A.O.C., also visited 13th Rifle Bde.	A/6
do	14/11/19		Usual routine work. Visited Concentration Camps at Gouzeaucourt and Montigny-aux-Pont — R.O.D. — A.M.P.D. Croisier and 55th 166 Station.	A/6
do	15/11/19		Usual Routine work. Visited Concentration Camps Montigny-aux-Pont. 1 and 4, 43 2nd Div., 38 to G.C.S.	A/6
do	16/11/19		Visited R.O.D., 376 Inf. Bn. — Detail 43 2nd Div. — Saw mill.	A/6
do	17/11/19		Usual routine work which is very heavy owing to preparations for Demobilization. Visited R.O.D. re/Scheme to send to sparts vehicles shortly coming in.	A/6

Army Form C. 2118.

WAR DIARY
or
INTELLIGENCE SUMMARY.
(Erase heading not required.)

Instructions regarding War Diaries and Intelligence Summaries are contained in F. S. Regs., Part II. and the Staff Manual respectively. Title pages will be prepared in manuscript.

Place	Date	Hour	Summary of Events and Information	Remarks and references to Appendices
Iposelles	18/1/19		Usual routine work. Attended conference at H.Q.	A/10
do	19/1/19		do do Visited 37th B.A.B and 153 Field Coy.	A/10
do	20/1/19		Visited 4th Division with G.O. R.E. M.B. also visited 8th, 9th, 10th Brigade H.Q. S.D.M. and R.E.O. respectively, returned by field Cashier way. Visited Corps and 37th Repair Coy.	A/10
do	21/1/19		Visited O.A.S. IV Corps and N.B. IV Corps troops	A/10
do	22/1/19		Usual routine work. Visited R.O.B. and Stables Sidings	A/10
do	23/1/19		Routine work very much on the increase - various repairs to ordnance motor lorry call for.	A/10
do	24/1/19		Visited IV Corps demobilization Camp - A.A and Q.M.G in camp. Chadwick is in charge. Saw required to send vehicles into same are returned on demobilization. Visited R.M.O	A/10

Place	Date	Hour	Summary of Events and Information	Remarks and references to Appendices
Roselies	26/11/19		Usual routine work. Visit H.Q. & field Ambulance	A/B
do	27/11/19		Visited Corps troops Issuing and R.E. - the latter having exposed from Army re shortage of Boots in the unit	A/B
do	28/11/19		Visited Divi Laundry re. a clean clothing issue to now arrival of March to 5,550 disposals from 16 Divn 19th inst	A/B
do	29/11/19		Usual routine work. Ammunition Column and Machine Gun Park Areas recommendation for stores returns re demobilization	A/B
do	30/11/19		Proceeded on 14 days leave to England. Visited R.E.	A/B

WAR DIARY FOR

FEBRUARY - 1919.

DEPUTY ASSISTANT DIRECTOR OF ORDNANCE SERVICES.
~~37XXAE~~XXXXXXXXXXXXXXXXXXXXX

37 th DIVISION.

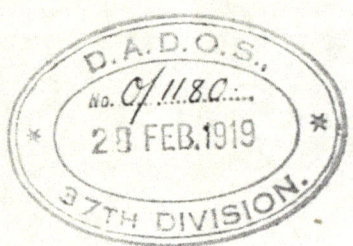

Army Form C. 2118.

WAR DIARY
or
INTELLIGENCE SUMMARY.
(Erase heading not required.)

Place	Date	Hour	Summary of Events and Information	Remarks and references to Appendices
Goalie	20/1/19		Returned from leave	A/G
do	21/1/19		Usual routine work. Demobilisation work very heavy. Staff very full with up store & returned equipment—about 30 truck loads. This matter has been taking up both A.D.S & Army's acting for authority to despatch to Base.	A/G
do			As there is no room to receive same.	
do	22/1/19		Interviews with A.O.D. IV Corps re demobilisation and general Ordnance matters. Great difficulty experienced in obtaining fatigue parties. Authority received to despatch one truck of up store per day to Base.	A/G
do	23/1/19		Visited R.O.D., A.O.D.P., 42nd Div'n and Ranforts in which equipment 37th Div will eventually be stored.	A/G
do	24/1/19		Attended conference at D.A.G. United Kingdoms up & down Div (4th Army & spare divns)	A/G
do	25/1/19		do do	A/G
			As to Utilization work very heavy	

WAR DIARY
or
INTELLIGENCE SUMMARY.

(Erase heading not required.)

Army Form C. 2118.

Place	Date	Hour	Summary of Events and Information	Remarks and references to Appendices
Moislies	20/5/19		Visited 13th KRRs and R.W.D. Attended conferences of II Corps re demobilisation instructions and its forwary as I.E.S. of the Barracks Charleroi for all ranks in IV Corps	A/O
do	21/5/19		Usual routine work & de. Attlegation went to W.O., I.Bttn. R.E. to men sent out to report to B.O.M.L and run for I.E.S. Charleroi	A/O
do	22/5/19		Attended conference of O.Cs & Quartermasters at Barracks Charleroi	A/O

WAR DIARY FOR FEBRUARY - 1919.

DEPUTY ASSISTANT DIRECTOR OF ORDNANCE SERVICES.

37th DIVISION.

WAR DIARY.

for

MARCH, 1919.

From:-

  D. A. D. ORDNANCE"
  37th DIVISION.

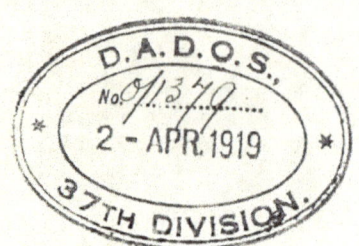

WAR DIARY
or
INTELLIGENCE SUMMARY.
(Erase heading not required.)

Army Form C. 2118.

Vol 43

Place	Date	Hour	Summary of Events and Information	Remarks and references to Appendices
Spostes	1/3/19.		Usual routine work. Visited R.O.B, Chapel 42nd Div. and factory at Corneille - note new German Ammunition to store	A/6
do	2/3/19.		Visited 37th M.-2. Coy. Naval H.Q 2nd Div. re demobilization instructions and G.G. at Chalons	A/6
do	3/3/19.		Usual routine and demobilization work. Circulars etc and L to all by car	A/6
do	4/3/19.		Whole day given to clearing up of burglar, honduran, Costaura etc	A/6
do	5/3/19		Usual routine work as do. Visited Ordnance Ammn personnel at Corneille - Motte	A/6
do	6/3/19		Visited 37. In Repy - U.A.S.Q.- R.O.D.- and R.O.D.	A/6
do	7/3/19		Usual routine work. Visited 28 In. 1st Div.	A/6
do	8/3/19		Ammunition etc despatched to bons in Box Car (Asch consignment) Visited D. Chopal 42nd Div re L.O.S.	A/6
do	9/3/19		Usual routine and demobilization work	A/6
do	10/3/19		Ottewells with Ourdname equipment committee	A/6

WAR DIARY
or
INTELLIGENCE SUMMARY.

Army Form C. 2118.

Place	Date	Hour	Summary of Events and Information	Remarks and references to Appendices
Spa Belgium	11/3/19		Usual routine work. Visited DADOS & Dir R.A.O. Pre DDS, and S of S Chateau	A/O
do	12/3/19		Usual routine work. Visited 37th Inf.B re movement to Rhine	A/O
do	13/3/19		Usual routine & demobilization work	A/O
do	14/3/19		do. do. Attended 4th Army Equipment Conference	A/O
do	15/3/19		Attended conference at S of S Chateau re wheels and R.O.D. re Laundry trucks	A/O
do	16/3/19		Usual routine work. Visited 37th DAC	A/O
do	17/3/19		do do. Visited 9th A. Staff, our Laundry	A/O
do	18/3/19		Attended conference at D.H.Q. Visited by AA & QMG IV in the afternoon	A/O
do	19/3/19		Visited DADOS & Dir our R.A.O. and IV Corps H.S.	A/O
do	20/3/19		Inspecting Unit's equipment at S.S. Chateau during morning. Afternoon office work	A/O

WAR DIARY
or
INTELLIGENCE SUMMARY.

Army Form C. 2118.

Place	Date	Hour	Summary of Events and Information	Remarks and references to Appendices
Spoelie	21/3/19		Inspected Units equipment at C.R.S. Chateau	A/6
do	22/3/19		do do do	A/6
do	23/3/19		Usual routine work. Visited 37th Inf Bn.	A/6
do	24/3/19		do do Visited NM 99¾ I de R/4D and	A/6
do	25/3/19		142 Heavy batty R/4D. Sends Incidents & Mob. Tables from some units received and signed. Representative from 4th Army Officers Clothing Depot, Amiens visited S.A.S.D. with stores for officers requiring same.	A/6
do	26/3/19		Usual routine work. Inspected ups stores of Artillery Pks	A/6
do	27/3/19		Visited 37th D.ab. - 37th Bn h/4B. 37th Div Train	A/6
do	28/3/19		Visited R.S.D., R.E.O - wants 43rd Div- and D&L Chardier	A/6
do	29/3/19		Usual routine work. Demobilization Lectures very heavy	A/6
do	30/3/19		do do went through Demob Incidents with O/C 9 th A. Staff as they were excessive	A/6

Army Form C. 2118.

WAR DIARY
or
INTELLIGENCE SUMMARY.
(Erase heading not required.)

Place	Date	Hour	Summary of Events and Information	Remarks and references to Appendices
Poelus	2/3/19		Heavy rain all day. Visited 37 & 39 M.G.B. in defensive work. Watch J.S. Attended conference at IX Corps "Q" Branch, Chateau.	A/6

WAR DIARY FOR APRIL 1919

FROM.

D. A. D. O. S., 37th DIVISION.

WAR DIARY
or
INTELLIGENCE SUMMARY.
(Erase heading not required.)

Army Form C. 2118.

Place	Date	Hour	Summary of Events and Information	Remarks and references to Appendices
Apollo	1/4/19		Usual routine work. Rep. from Officers Clothing Depot Arras attached.	A/6
do	2/4/19		Routine and demobilization work any heavy frequent heavy arrangements for Heavy Artillery nearby attending.	A/6
do	3/4/19		Visited R.O.D - Surplus vehicle Park and 37th M. Amy - O.S + th Auto.	A/6
do	4/4/19		Usual routine work. DHQ moved to Charleroi. Visited old 37th Div train is now to take vehicles from which Park to Ruthen	A/6
do	5/4/19		Visited S. army IV Corps demob:- R.O.B - 豆 L.O.S Charleroi and surplus vehicle park, and D.H.Q. Surplus vehicles not moved as arranged owing to wrong instructions being given by HQ Army Issue. Arrangements made with Div Train to have vehicles removed on 6th inst	A/6
do	6/4/19		Usual routine work	A/6
do	7/4/19		Returns of stores surplus to Esst: table of Heavy Art: attached very unreliable. Great difficulty experienced with return of returned stores owing to this being frequently at local althoughts and new attached to D.A.D.O.S having to be returned to Units Units	A/6

Army Form C. 2118.

WAR DIARY
or
INTELLIGENCE SUMMARY.
(Erase heading not required.)

Instructions regarding War Diaries and Intelligence Summaries are contained in F. S. Regs., Part II. and the Staff Manual respectively. Title pages will be prepared in manuscript.

Place	Date	Hour	Summary of Events and Information	Remarks and references to Appendices
Ypsoles	8/4/19		Routine and demobilyzation work	A/6
do	9/4/19		Visited IV Corps Demob - Staff kept Heavy Art - and D.N.O.	A/6
do	10/4/19		Usual routine and demobilyzation work - several storms 9/10 98 submitted for expiration. Returns of artillery clips from Heavy artillery attached amt me to 9/10 98 very heavy.	A/6
do	11/4/19		Usual routine work	A/6
do	12/4/19		Attended conference of D.A.Ds O.S of diff Areas at 10 a.m. area Headquarters	A/6
do	13/4/19		Usual routine work. Visited O.S # 8th Full Amble re demob. In duck	A/6
do	14/4/19		Visited div H.Q. I.b.C. Chartres, Horse Horses and O.6 i.34 Employment Coy. Made statius to return to UK	A/6
do	15/4/19		Office work very heavy owing to Units speaking up	A/6
do	16/4/19		Visited R.O.D - arr. Heavy unbio - saved chateau and ik Col: of Brat and amm	A/6

Army Form C. 2118.

WAR DIARY
or
INTELLIGENCE SUMMARY.

(Erase heading not required.)

Instructions regarding War Diaries and Intelligence Summaries are contained in F. S. Regs., Part II. and the Staff Manual respectively. Title pages will be prepared in manuscript.

Place	Date	Hour	Summary of Events and Information	Remarks and references to Appendices
Apache	17/4/19		Usual routine and demobilisation work	A/6
do	18/4/19		Visited Div HQ - White Park. OC 37th Div Milty - RWD and OC RE Thakur	A/6
do	19/4/19		Visited various Batteries. S/L Chalmers 37th Div tid Hill Batavia Area and do so field Batteries	A/6
do	20/4/19		Easter Sunday - work suspended as far as possible	A/6
do	21/4/19		Divl. Headquarters left for England. Visited enemy wheel dump at Menappe. 9 a/tos 37th Divn. attempted Batavia Sub Area and retains Ordnance removed	A/6
do	22/4/19		Attended conference of A/Capt.Is sub area at Corps Headquarters	A/6

WAR   DIARY

FOR

APRIL   1919.

FROM:-

D. A. D. O. S.   BRABANT SUB-AREA
(No. 4 AREA.)

WAR DIARY
or
INTELLIGENCE SUMMARY.
(Erase heading not required.)

Army Form C. 2118.

Instructions regarding War Diaries and Intelligence Summaries are contained in F. S. Regs., Part II. and the Staff Manual respectively. Title pages will be prepared in manuscript.

Place	Date	Hour	Summary of Events and Information	Remarks and references to Appendices
Mons	22/4/19		Attended conference of D.A.D.O.S. of Sub Areas at Corps Headquarters.	A/6
do	23/4/19		Visited O.O. the Mortuaries taking of surplus stores from stores and personnel being transferred. Visited Brabant Sub Area H.Q.	A/6 A/6
do	24/4/19		Visited various dumps and Brabant Sub Area with D.A.D.O.S.	A/6
do	25/4/19		Visited A.D.O.S. Canadian Corps re vehicles to be handed over by Canad. 4th Canadian Div	A/6
do	26/4/19		Visited D.A.D.O.S Canadian 4th Div re vehicles and re dump at Point St Etienne	A/6
do	27/4/19		Visited Brabant Sub Area H.Q. and Ch. S. Charleroi	A/6
do	28/4/19		Attended conference D.A.D.S. Sub Area H.Q.	A/6
do	29/4/19		Visited Bredoux Sub Area H.Q. and gun park Houdeng	A/6
do			- do - do and D.A.D.O.S. Ammunition	A/6
do	30/4/19		Officer to Sub Area reported	A/6

WAR DIARY
FOR APRIL 1918.

FROM:-

D.A.D.O.S. BRABANT SUB-AREA
(No. 4 AREA.)

WAR DIARY FOR APRIL 1919

FROM

D. A. D. O. S., 37th DIVISION.